The Scent of Odisha

Talkings

Charudutta's eclectic anthology, *The Scent of Odisha* is a wonderful window to the extraordinary cultural and natural treasures of the state. I am sure many readers, even Odia readers, will be inspired to explore this corder of India after reading it"
Sanjeev Sanyal
Internationally Acclaimed Economist & Bestselling Writer

All about Odisha, coming from Charudutta, the multi-faceted public intellectual, *The Scent of Odisha* is a trendsetter in many ways. Gripping, smart and up to date. Almost everything about real Odisha for a global audience.
Padma Shri Binapani Mohanty
*Distinguished Litterateur from Odisha,
Founder Odisha Lekhika Sansad*

In Odisha, we hardly have somebody with your perspective and your perceptions of modernity. Charudutta you are the most eligible chronicler of the current Odia cultural scene. More power to your enquiries. The *Scent of Odisha* is a treat.
Devdas Chhotray
Indian Odia author, Administrator and Academician. The first vice-chancellor of Ravenshaw University

The Scent of Odisha is a precious lens, watching Odisha as it moves from the art forms, the economy, social welfare to the civil society and all its elements. Charudutta, the erudite Odisha aesthete, is global. This book is for keeps, for times to come. It breathes Odisha, every breath.
Padma Shri Dr Mohan Agashe
Actor and a Doctor. Recipient of Sangeet Natak Academy Award

A public intellectual, Charudutta is intensely involved in Odisha development and the book has embodied all hues and nuances of Odisha in a rare digest. *The Scent of Odisha* plays cupid, you would love Odisha, if you haven't, still. The book is an intimate affair with Odisha.

Padma Shri Aruna Mohanty
Odissi exponent, aesthete, visiting scholar Cornell University, IIT

This book, *The Scent of Odisha* is a must read and is a rare treat on Odisha and a reference book for all. Charudutta Panigrahi is Odisha's emissary.

Dr. Sukant K. Mohapatra
Scientist, Founder Chairman, National Institute of Science and Technology (NIST)

The *Scent of Odisha* is a starburst of a book, brilliant broad sweep, rare. One which talks about Odisha at an international level. Charudutta is a remarkable populariser.

Sukanta Sahu
New Age Entrepreneur and Social Leader in UK.
Global promoter of Odia culture.

The Scent of Odisha

Charudutta Panigrahi

BLACK EAGLE BOOKS
2021

BLACK EAGLE BOOKS

USA address:
7464 Wisdom Lane
Dublin, OH 43016

India address:
E/312, Trident Galaxy, Kalinga Nagar,
Bhubaneswar-751003, Odisha, India

E-mail: info@blackeaglebooks.org
Website: www.blackeaglebooks.org

First International Edition Published by
BLACK EAGLE BOOKS, 2021

THE SCENT OF ODISHA
by Charudutta Panigrahi

Original Copyright © **Charudutta Panigrahi**

All rights reserved. No part of this publication may be reproduced, stored in a retrieval system, or transmitted, in any form or by any means, electronic, mechanical, photocopying, recording or otherwise without the prior permission of the publisher.

Cover & Interior Design: Ezy's Publication

ISBN- 978-1-64560-149-4 (Paperback)
Library of Congress Control Number: 2021931168

Printed in United States of America

To
Koraput
the wonderland

Preface

The *Scent of Odisha* ought to travel far and wide, not only because the Odisha musk needs olfactors but the universe requires it to live better. My mother, Mandakini Panigrahi was the reason for my unflinching Odisha espousal, a natural augmentation of mother with motherland. For hours we used to think & talk about places, people, trends, past, present and the future of the civilisation. She was a prolific writer, a known progressive mind and an incorrigible optimist. Positivity is deep seated in my genes and it flowers incessantly, piqued by the abundance in the state. Overwhelming naturalness & credulity, which is why some believe that it is a mystic land. Has to be. The unimaginable & incredible happens in Odisha, defying calculations, assertions and wily aggressions. Odisha carries a great mystery within itself which has to be realised and a great potentiality which has to be actualised.

Hence *the Scent of Odisha* is peculiar and quite different and yet not mulish. Scent knows no border and Odias know no delimitation. This cosmopolitanism of Odisha has a fragrance which has both the high and low notes, the steadfast & discursive narratives, the ingenue & chic souls and all the variants to make it a full-bodied fragrance. I and many I know, discuss about Odisha, pigeonholed to a few oft repeated topics - the ballyhoo of poverty, the rigmarole of Odissi, the inevitability of natural disasters and the helplessness of migration. But there is much more to Odisha – the youth brimming with contemporary thinking, the serendipity of brilliance in unknown quarters, the upswing of the economy, the promising industrialisation and most crucial, the response of common man to sudden changes around them. My work with the communities both at the remote locations and at policy tables has prompted a 360 view on where the idyllic land is headed, in an absolutely clear sighted and accessible manner. Odisha is a world in itself, and an all-encompassing spectrum. Not that I am bewitchingly infatuated, but I wish you sway with Odisha consciousness which would open many closed minds for you and all of us. The essays in *the Scent* are ajar windows waiting to be stretched open. The thoughts, experiences, intrigues, emotions, angst, celebrations in the essays are the cues.

The enormity & diversity of Odisha canvas is daunting, and the *Scent* is a whiff around the wood. Much lies inside it. The dedication of the book to Koraput celebrates the simplicity and richness of my indigenous community. It is here that everything has started, even fourteen billion years ago and it is here that the next centuries are being crafted. My reflection in the essay, *Origin of the Origin* will speak more on this. *Akshaya Mohanty* deserved more from his fans, *Madhu babu's* nationalism should be *au courant* with generations, a *Ministry of thinking* is perhaps essential now and the unscrupulous *Officers* can't be allowed to derail progress. Many more waves rough out in the tranquil Buddha land, a gem in the east, where the Sun rises a bit early, every day. Every day Odisha has a new story and every day Odisha fetes the past. This swing is the romance of *the Scent*, the mystic spirit, maverick, uncorked but also corked. Inclusive of all shades but much beyond the ideas of right & wrong.

You are my co-traveller now, my *khati* mate. Let's meet atop the blue mountain, floating with the divine breeze at Koraput. It is extant & pulsating.

Charudutta Panigrahi

CONTENTS

Koraput, The Alchemy Land	15
'Origin Of The Origin' (Part I)	16
Origin Of The Origin (Part II)	20
Origin Of The Origin (Part III)	25
Intellectualism & Odisha	28
"Mo Sarkar" In Odisha Can Be A Global Model	36
Migrant's Heart	41
Odissi For The World	46
CSR & Atmanirbhar Bharat	52
The Silence Of The Energy & The Enigma	58
Covid -19 & Utkal Divas 2020	64
Science Of Internalisation	70
Central University Of Odisha	74
The Companies Need To Internalise CSR	79
Father & Father Figure	84
Gram Sabha & India's Future	87
The Verandas Of Kala Bhoomi	96
Silence Of Civil Society	99
Samuel Sahu (Babi)	103
The Art Of Destroying Bhubaneswar	105
Theatre In Odisha	111
Social Distancing & Khatti	122
Save Koraput : The Wonderland	126
Social Work's Diminishing Returns	138
Micro Planning In Odisha, Post- Covid	143
We Have Failed Mr. Akshaya Mohanty	148
Mission "Clean Puri"	151
The Devdas Effect	154
Mines Reservation & Odisha's Bargain	158
True Independence & Nep 2020	162
On JPD	167

Kotia Panchayat Is Our Family	172
Odisha 2036	177
Sailing Away…	189
Odisha Budget: Climate Change	192
Sarbeswar, the born crusader	196
The Future Of Start-ups In Odisha	199
Rangabati And Much Beyond	205
Odisha's Biggest Gamble	210
Rumi In Konark	216
Primary School Dropouts In Rayagada District	219
India's Freedom Movement Against NPOs	225
God & Climate Emergency	230
Art & Life In Odisha	237
Meeting Mr Mehta	243
Nostalgia - Smruti Tume…	246
Strangely There Is No Airport At Brahmapur, Odisha	248
Odisha Preparing For High Speed Growth – New RI Cirlces	252
Ministry Of Thinking	256
New Year 2021, New Chief Secretary	261
Balakrushna Dash – The Renaissance Man Of Odia Music	267
The Chronic Odia Self-denigration	171
Mani, Sanyam & Divinity In Puri	276
When Do Politicians Get To Think?	281
Why Are We Scared Of Tribals?	287
Ode To Thy Spirit!	292
Say Aum Jagannath Instead Of Jai Jagannath	293

Koraput, the *alchemy* land

Koraput, the beauty
sans guile,
is the divine soil
for generations,
the genesis of humanity,
amidst my brooks and nature's stockpile
(Koraput, the blessed land & the future of Asia)

'ORIGIN of the ORIGIN'

The search started when someone asked me, " Who is Lord Jagannath and What is the origin?". I believe that the research could only be at the surface as, every deep dive to unearth, felt like surface. I was pitted against infinite and mystic which I trust has created everything that we see and which we don't see. Hence I named the write as "Origin of the Origin" which is a never ending loop, which defies time and space and is unanalysable. At this point, at the very gate of the infinite, I have to leave science. This is where science becomes mere "mortal" or perishable. And the quest begins from here onwards.

**ado yaddaru plavate sindhoh pare apurusham,
tadarabhasya durhano tena gacchaparastaram,**

"In the beginning, the primeval Lord manifested as the transcendental Daru Brahman on the shore of the Ocean, and those who go to take shelter in this Supreme Lord are sheltered from all difficulties."

10th mandala (10.155.3) of the Rig Veda

Prior to being placed at the 12th century temple at Puri built by Choda Ganga Deva, Lord Jagannath was most probably worshipped at the sea shore. (Sanskrit Scholar Murari Mishra has referred to this in a 9th Century play

Anargharaghav Natakam: Reference: Orissa Historical Journal, Vol III, No I PP.9-10).

Lord Jagannath is MahaVishnu and the epic poet Sarala Das (of Pratarudradeva's time) had described Lord Jagannath as an Avataree and not an Avatar. He is not an incarnation. So, he doesn't have any life story or leelas or plays as any other Avatar like Rama & Krishna. MahaVishnu is an address which signifies the high pedestal of Lord Jagannath which signifies that He is the highest form of Vishnu. Avatars (incarnation) of Vishnu, all spring from Him.

In the Utkala Khanda of the Skanda Purana there is a question raised "In which yuga or era did Indradyumna establish his kingdom at Purushottama kshetra?"

kasminyuge sat u nripa indradyumnobhavanmune?

The answer says it all: (in Utkala Khanda)
asit krutayugevipra indradyumnomahanrupaha suryavamsesa dharmatmastasthu panchamapurusha.

"During Satyayuga, there was a great king, Indradyumna, who possessed all the noble qualities of a brahmana. He was born in Suryavamsa in the fifth generation from Brahma and was a very religious man."

There are multiple versions of the origin of the Lord but in the commonly accepted explanation it is said that in the first half of Brahma's life (parardha), the Lord took the form of Nila Madhava and appeared in Sankha Kshetra (in this conch shaped geography) in order to give His blessings to the sinners of this world. And In the second parardha (the first Satya Yuga of the first Manvantara), the king named Indradyumna or Indrasavarni was born as the fifth descendent of Brahma and ruled over the land of Malava, making his capital in Avanti (now Ujjain). Indradyumna is also known as

Avanti Naresh. He was a great devotee of Vishnu and yearned to have the Lord's audience (darshan) which fructified when on the information of an ascetic (rishi) called Jatila, he sent his brother Vidyapati on a mission to locate Nila Madhav (the blue Lord), whom Indradyumna wanted to worship. Vidyapati located the Lord at the tribal land, amidst nature, worshipped by Visvavasu, and his tribal clan.

Interpretation: The meeting of Vidyapati and Visvavasu represents unique unity in diversity – Vidyapati representing the princely and brahminical (he was the Rajguru) perspective and Visvavasu as the tribal (people of nature) chief. The Lord's worship and the temple proceedings are seamless blending of two diverse cultures i.e. the brahminical Aryan tradition and the tribal Sabara cultures joined to form the unique tradition of the Vratyas. The Daitas (believed to be from the tribal descendance and the Patis (from the brahmanical origin) form the principal set of servitors of the Lord who exemplify non-dogmatic worship of the Lord – Lord belongs to everyone in the universe & beyond and not confined to any orthodoxy in worship or practices.

Vidyapati was overwhelmed after having the divine look (darshan) at the form of Nila Madhava, and had to return to Avanti, his kingdom, albeit against his wish of staying back with the Nila Madhava. Such was his devotion for Nila Madhava that as soon as Vidyapati left Purushottama kshetra, Nila (Indranilamani) Madhava and Rohini kunda vanished from their original places. But Visvavasu had mentioned to Vidyapati that Nila Madhava would show up in a different form and he need not be saddened by the thought that he could no more have the divine vision of the Lord (Nila Madhava). As per the Indranilamani Purana Vidyapati narrated to Indradyumna his journey to and arrival in Purushottama kshetra, where he witnessed the presence of Devas (the other celestial Lords and angels) and their preparations for performing secret rituals for Nilamadhava. Guided by Visvavasu, he went to the Rohini kunda, where he, Vidyapati, took bath and meditated under the Kalpa Bata. After the Lord's services were completed, the Devas returned to the heavens (Svargaloka) and Vidyapati on his return described Nila Madhava to Indradyumna, his brother, as 'the Lord of the Universe, 81 angulas (fingers) tall and the divine figure standing on a golden lotus flower. So spellbound was Indradyumna on hearing this that he promised to shift his capital to Purushottama kshetra and dedicate his life to Lord Jagannatha, He declared his wishes as,

tatravasam karisyamipurvadurgani chaivahi, satopacharahe srinatham pujayishyedinedine
"There I will make my residence as I had already decided, and there I am going to perform perfect ritual worship to the Lord every day."

Origin of the Origin

(Part II)

The King arranged to go to Purushottama kshetra with all the residents of Avanti, and the departure day was fixed on sukla paksha sasthi in the month of Jyestha, on a Wednesday. This day is still celebrated as Sitala Sasthi in the Jagannatha temple and the anniversary day of Shiva's marriage; on this day Madana mohana and Shiva (in the form of Pancha Pandavas: Lokanatha, Yamesvara, Nilakantha, Kapalamochana and Markandesvara) feast together. According to the Vana Parva of Mahabharata, it is believed that the Pandavas reached Puri on this day for the first time alongwith Lord Krishna to get the Darshan (divine grace) of Purushottama, and they stayed for three days. As stated in the Indranilamani Purana, King Indradyumna was accompanied by Narada Muni, four brahmanas each expert in one of the Vedas, two body guards, one minister, the Queen, and four trusted friends. These fourteen-people constituted the royal entourage from Avanti (the modern Ujjain in Madhya Pradesh), After crossing Mahanadi and visiting many Devas and Devis (goddesses) like charchika and others, the entourage reached river Gandhabaha where the king heard divine sounds of mantras being chanted, and was under the assumption that he had reached Purushottama kshetra. However, Narada Muni explained to the King that he had arrived at Ekamra kshetra (today's Bhubaneswar), which had been created by Sri Vishnu with His Sudarshana chakra when He rested here as Ananta Vasudeva after killing the demons.

Narada Muni advised the King to take bath in the Bindu Sarovara and have the audience of Ananta Vasudeva and Lingaraja. Lingaraj or Lord Shiva blessed Indradyumna and spoke to him about the glories of Purushottama kshetra, telling him also that He resides in Purushottam kshetra as the Astha Sambhu (Shiva in eight forms).

Indradyumna visited other places like Belesvara, Nilakanthesvara under the guidance of Margadevi (Batamangala) on his way to Purushottam Kshetra but was aghast to learn that Nilamadhava had disappeared after been seen by Vidyapati. But Narada comforted the King, saying that the King would have the great fortune of installing the Nila Madhav Deity, but in order to be able to see Indranilamani Madhava, the King were to first perform one thousand Ashvamedha yajnas (sacrifices). On completion of the Ashvamedha yajnas Nila Madhava appeared in a dream and informed the king that he would have to retrieve the sacred Daru from the ocean and prepare new Deities(forms) to be installed in a grand temple.

Interpretation: *Strange and mystic are the ways of the Lord. His designs are unfathomable for human minds. Since the Lord has come from Nature, He chose to remain 'organic' and rooted in nature. Jagannath is made up of a piece of Neem tree, what we call Daru or Mahadaru and the Lord is known as Daru Debata. The other deities are made up of clay, rock or metals. He is the Nature God for the Cosmos.*

It is believed that after Vidyapati's Darshana, the Indranilamani Madhava had disappeared into Patalaloka (the sub-land or the recess of below land surface). On this day of installation, during the Navakalevara ritual the descendants of Vidyapati belonging to the Kaundinya gotra move the nabhi brahma (considered as the Indranilamani) from the old Deities to the new ones, to be made from the sacred Daru from the ocean.

Guided by the dream, the King and his party started climbing the Nilachala hill, arrived at Kalpa Bata and had the audience (Darshana) of Adi Narsimha. Indradyumna was instructed to worship Adi Narasimha and installed the Deity of Narsimha as the ista deva (presiding Lod) of the yajna (sacrifice). Without the endorsements of Narsimha, the yajna couldn't have been performed and nor the Lord installed and consecrated.

The yajna was performed in a kunda (holy pit) 14 x 7 hasta (about 7 x 3.5 feet) wide, according to the specifications (for the Vaishnava Samskaras). The yajna ceremony was so detailed and grand that it was unprecedented for any of the yugas, and even the established Purushottama kshetra the most important kshetra/location of the universe. The night before the last day of the yajna, Indradyumna had a dream in which he had the visualisation of the form of Jagannatha. Balabhadra, Subhadra and Sudarshana and the day as per the tithi (the oracle calendar) was Asadha sukla Navami, which is celebrated as Sandhya Darshana (Indradyumna Mahotsava) during the annual Ratha Yatra festival.

The king's exotic dream can be described as:

diptam balarka-koti prabhamanalashikamsapta-
jihvagrajvalam
madhyesubhram prashantam phanimukuta
manishobhitam kamapalam
tanmadhyeshankrachakranalinavala gadan
dharinamlakshminathan
bhadramalingya vakhyamapasyan rupa tan
saccidanandarupam (Skanda Purana)

"Among the seven radiating tongues of Agni, that appeared to be brighter than thousands of new Suns, in the centre, he saw Kamapalam Balabhadra, white in color with a peaceful expression and a crown of snakes decorated with gem stones. In the centre he saw the Lord of Lakshmi Devi (Lakshminatha), holding sankha, chakra, gada and padma and embracing Subhadra on the left side of His chest. Sudarshan appeared as the radiance around Them."

The yajna ceremony continued for ten days, at the end of which, the King distributed many cows and other gifts to the invitees, especially to the brahmanas. Following the rituals minutely, (as per the Soma yajna paddhati or procedure), king Indradyumna accompanied by his queen completed the avabhrita snana in the Mahodadhi (the ocean) in the place that is famous as Rakta tirtha or Chakra tirtha, which falls between Bilvesvara in the north and the Mahavedi in the south. The Deities installed at this place (now known as Chakra Narasimha temple) are Chakra Narasimha, Adi Narasimha, and Lakshmi Narasimha.

As soon as the bath ceremony was completed, a huge log of wood arrived on the shore, its roots still pointing to the ocean. The tree was marked with the symbols of the chakra and sankha, and it was coiled by ethereal and exotic shrubs and plants with fragrance. Narada explained that this huge log was one hair of Vishnu from Svetadvipa. The Daru (the sacred log) was taken to the Adapamandapa (the place of the yajna or the yajnasala) at the present day Gundicha. The Daru was worshipped at the spot and when Indradyumna asked Narada Muni about the shape and form of the Lord to be carved from the from the log, Narada replied that it was up to the Lord and His commandments and as is His wont, a voice from beyond said:

suguptayammahavedyamsvayamso'avatarisyati prachadyatamdinanyosah jabat panchadashani vai

"This log of wood has come to be installed on the Mahavedi as per its own wish. You must seal this area completely for the next fifteen days."

■

Origin of the Origin

(Part III)

It was magical and at that time a frail old man appeared and requested the King to be taken into the Karusala (workshop), emphasising that he was going to carve the Deities. The old man (who was Visvakarma, the architect and craftsman of the heavenly planets) said he would carve the Deities, but his condition was that he should not be disturbed in his work and as he would be working in a secluded room behind closed doors, and no one was to be allowed to enter the room for the next fifteen days. And outside the Karusala there should be musicians playing all the time so that the sound of the carving work does not travel out. Day after day, Vishwakarma worked diligently with immaculate planning and work, layer after layer. But the King could not resist the temptation to see the work of Vishwakarma and the Lord's forms, opened a window and was trying to peep into the work of Vishwakarma stealthily, when he looked back, saw the King and in a split moment turned into a mass of light and assimilated into the idols of the Lords, which remained unfinished ever since.

Patience is one of the greatest virtues to be pursued by humanity and the King's impatience stopped the idol work and prevented the divine dexterity of Vishwakarma, from reaching completion.

Story of the temple:

Narada advised the King to construct a temple on the Nilachala hill which was to be a thousand hasta (hands which was 500 foot) long. And after the completion of the temple, Indradyumna decided to invite Brahma for the consecration ceremony of the Deities.

The King left for Brahmaloka to call on Brahma and extend the invitation. However, he was stopped at the gate by a guard named Manikodara because Indradyumna appeared human with a material body. But with the intervention of Narada, both were allowed. Brahma gladly accepted the invitation, instructing the King to commence the arrangements and committing his active participation. As Indradyumna had had to wait one day in Brahmaloka before being allowed to see Brahma, a complete Manvantara (a cycle of 71 maha yugas, equivalent to 4,320,000 earthly years) had passed on Prithviloka (the planet Earth). And in this Manvantara the temple structure had caved in and was sunk below the sand. In the absence of Indradyumna, the then king of Utkala, Gala Madhava, had the temple resurrected and pulled out and claimed deceitfully to have built the temple himself.

On Indradyumna's return there was widespread confusion. But Kaka Bhusundi, the ageless, Rama devotee crow living on the sacred banyan tree near the temple, in its inimitable style told everyone the true story about Gala Madhav.

But Indradyumna accepted Gala Madhava as an associate, despite his folly and declared that that Gala

Madhava would be welcome to worship Jagannatha together with him, and that the Deity installed by Gala Madhava would also be worshiped on the main altar as one of the seven main Deities of the temple. This Deity is called Nila Madhava and is worshipped on the Ratna Singhasana till date.

ya esa plavate daruh sindhu pare hyapaurushah, tamupasyaduraradhyam muktimyati sudurlabham

"One who venerates that transcendental piece of wood that floated to the ocean shore, which is so hard to worship properly, will attain the rarest form of salvation."

Utkala Khanda of Skanda Purana (21.3)

(Major references: Utkala Khanda of Kapil Samhita and Madala Panji, compilation of Shishu Krishna Das in the 18th century in Oriya language under the title Deula tola)

Intellectualism & Odisha

Like GDP, IQ should not be regarded as a comprehensive measure – GDP of human development and IQ of intellectualism. In the last 100 years the general IQ of humanity has increased about 30 points – about 3 points every decade. Compared to 1920, we all are geniuses and our brain sizes have increased almost 3 times since bipedal apes, Australopithecus. Today our brains consume one-fifth of our calorie intake. So what? In Odisha, group living, and group thinking has been in the upswing since the 90's. Certainly there is increasing cognitive demands due to the drastically changing social dynamics. For those in their 30's, unprecedented spurt in educational institutes, increasing access to public services, exponential increase in disposable income, unbridled consumerism, and virtually free ride in the technology highway have made information usable like never before. But the usage of information hovers primarily around products and services with extremely short life utility. New product takes over, bringing with it a wave of new information which again dies before it fully lives. This is the constant 'high' of consumerism. The below 30's are constantly hooked and occupied with trends. But we need original thinking and intellectualism. The future of Odisha should evolve as researchers, artists, technologists, and philosophers.

For half a century and more, Sachi Routray, Manoj Das, Ramakant Rath, Sitakant Mohapatra, Jagannath Prasad Das, Devdas Chotray, Haraprasad Das, Binapani Mohanty, Pratibha Ray continue to be the flag bearers of Odia literature. The style of Odia writing in general, remains unprovoked. Have we stopped thinking? Akhil Patnaik, Nandini Devi tried to bring in short, crisp form of writing and translation with gusts of fresh air. Jagyanseni of Pratibha Ray does a self-portrait of Panchali, with new lens and has appealed nationally. Jayant Mahapatra is the lone reaper, in English poems. But Odia literature, not all but mostly, is regional, cocooned in its own tidings and perilously uninspiring and dated. Konark, the mast as well as the touchstone of our thoughts, writings & backdrops, needs respite to breathe, to stand on its own feet, and collect from collapsing. Since 12th century, it has served & saved us. Non-filmy albums, or *laghu sangeet*, as we call, and puja releases have stopped after Khoka bhai. Barring Kadambini, all literary magazines, including the iconic Jhankara, are out of print or cease to exist or are reduced to lame mementos with token publications. "Why I stand for meetings" in college elections are now avoidable. Once upon a time, they thundered with the manifestos of young leaders-in-the-making. Mock UN Assemblies are the leadership simulation programs available at only a few, high end schools, which is the privilege of a few, very few. The below 35's are forming opinions, solely influenced by social media. No other media or source reaches them. They live in a world of their own. Elise Boulding, the famous sociologist once said something which is relevant to our current state. "If one is mentally out of breath all the time from dealing with the present, there is no energy left for imagining the future,". Where is the imagining?

We are living in the best of times but if we cut that time into slices, we realise that in every slice the period is getting shorter. Short-termism is the new venom. The next generation(s) are unable to look beyond this minute news cycle – a moment to -moment, temporal exhaustion. We, the seniors have to customise the legacy we want to leave behind. Only then it would serve its purpose to them and their future generations.

Intellectualism in Odisha has staggered, post 80's. Have we stopped ideating?

Today Odisha has poetry portals, storytelling sessions, non-bureaucrats giving full time time to literature, hordes of celebrity writers and thinkers making frequent jaunts to the state, internet giving equal opportunities for Khariar and Bhubaneswar to be informed and above all about 5 or more people in every 10 using internet in Odisha. A few years ago, in places like Bolangir, Aska, Nilagiri, Bhawanipatna, Rayagada, Malkangiri, Bhandaripokhari, evening soirees (read khati) of prominent citizens (not necessarily the rich and well heeled only) included intense conversations on local stories, political dramas in the state, the local college politics, and brainstorming on development. There are no citizen meetings now, except the likes of members' meets on fixed days by Rotary or Lions. Even though we all are on social media, throughout the day watching mindless videos and postings, we never care to pause and think for ourselves. When was the last I had spent time thinking (anything for that matter except my immediate material needs)? There are no central reference personalities which people can follow - some peer leaders, erudite celebrities who can promote 'thinking'. Odisha has enviable soft skills. Odias often describe themselves as reticent, introvertish. This is a strength rather than a weakness. Our quiet nature empowers us to engage with the world – but on our own terms. I have spoken to a lot of super successful Odias and they all started quiet, seemingly shy, and outwardly withdrawn. This unobtrusiveness is our strength. We are blessed because of our comity and we could use this as a strong mark. This strength does not come easily, anywhere in the world. Since that is our valuable genetic inheritance, can we describe it in an epithet like " Nirmaya Odia"/(ନିର୍ମାୟା ଓଡ଼ିଆ). Our divinity has dissuaded us from *maya* and hence the rat race is not for us. Our natural ability to intellectualise has been under utilised even with all the tools to wisdom are easily and equally available to all. When Odias go out they do well, is a catchphrase in every discussion on this this topic. If it is so, then why? Because of the eco system they get outside to provide many lateral approaches to the inherent quality of "Nirmaya Odia" they are brimming with. I would not lose hope if there are no billionaires in Odisha or if the quality of life is only measured in SGDP. There is no measure for aggregate life skills, something like a State Gross Soft Skills (SGSS). Everything in life starts with soft skills, we are the reservoir of them and yet go unrecognised. This is where I think intellectualism and nationalism overlap.

Can we institutionalise intellectualism in Odisha?

Hinglish communication with a strange twist of Odia is staple for the youth today. The parents do not mind as long as they look 'cool'. This 'cool quotient', slaying own language, is the bane of non-intellectualism of a state. Institutionalisation starts at home.

In the 50's Late Dr Mahatab organised Bishuba Milan

as a congregation of intellectuals in the state and the young writers and thinkers were recognised and publicised with hype. Hence it became a coveted felicitation and set a benchmark of quality writing and thinking. In all these years we have not had another thinkers' platform. We have many literary functions, but they are events heaping compliments on established superstars and most of them from outside. A young writer from Sonepur can not even enter the venue of the festival, which is always in a 5-star hotel in Bhubaneswar and with a clearly stratified invitee preference. The purpose of these multi-branded events is completely different, and no way contributes to the intellectual growth of the state. It might be good for event management and hospitality industry. Since *Gaan Majlis* (Village Parliament), a regular cartoon strip in Prajatantra has stopped, there has been no such sharp, incisive satire, every morning, to stir the state and set it thinking. The population of newspapers or dailies in Odisha is in all time high now but none of them carry interesting cartoons or snippets which would catch popular imagination. Now there are trained journalists and creative professionals available, like never before. In the mushrooming mass communication institutions including IIMC at Dhenkanal. The newspapers or e-Newspapers do not carry analytical pieces on policy or implementation issues. There are no windows which can open to 'thoughts'. The University of Culture or the other Universities should have department or stream, exclusively for *thinking*.

In Odisha, thinking should be new future and we can build a new Odisha.

Articles on our tribes and ethnicity are nothing but anthropological studies on tribals and marginalised people. The English used describes the writer more than the subject

– the frequent use of bombastic, obfuscate English to convey the scholastic supremacy of the writer. Even writings on our Lord Jagannath are unnecessarily complicated and complexly high sounding, be it in English or Odia. The articulation is much more significant that the writer. Intellectualism is far more important than the intellectuals –the sum is greater than the parts.

About 2-3 art foundations set up by successful senior artistes are operational in Odisha. Dinanath Pathy, Jatin Das, Jagannath Panda have set up foundations, but their residencies need greater support. Residencies could be the nurturing grounds for young minds from different districts of Odisha. Odisha is 27 more districts, other than Cuttack, Khordha and Puri and are full of talents. They need to be brought to the mainstream. Odissi, our marquee identity today needs life and rejuvenation. The Odissi research centre, since '86 has turned more to be an event centre rather than a research centre. With hardly any research or documentation being done, the centre is a popular event venue because of its vantage location, inexpensive charges, and good branding. Should we continue riding on Odissi without feeding it? Who is researching on new styles and presentations in Odissi? It is reduced to be only a passport to Padma awards.

In the present times new money from our rental economy has produced dilettantes. "Sponsorship" is the new key to convert a philistine to a cognoscenti. But this is a worldwide phenomenon. We should use this "patron" money to build our repertoire and make the art forms sustainable, however not get sucked into the super mart of culture.

Is our intellectualism peaking or has it already? There is a reverse trend globally. The IQ is showing signs of falling in countries like Finland, Norway, Denmark. In Odisha there is social stability, institutional opportunities, rich culture as reference and still we are deprived of inventiveness and originality. They say, no idea is original. But we can be inventive and intellectually entrepreneurial – invent new templates of poetry, literature, political analysis, cinematic production, scientific discoveries and above all our own thinking.

Here we need to clarify that IQ alone should not mean intellectualism. An intelligent person, with high IQ has the capacity, which is measurable, to think beyond, seek answers to curiosities and in the process develop own thoughts. The intellectual uses IQ to do all as mentioned above and additionally, disseminate.

After Pathani Samanta,(Mahamahopadhyaya Chandrasekhara Singha Harichandana Mahapatra Samanta), the great Indian astronomer in the league of Nicolaus Copernicus, Tycho Brahe, Johannes Kepler measured celestial distance and movements with the help of simple domestically used devices like bamboos and sticks. When he was a child, poor and unschooled, he could measure the number of vultures flying high and their velocity without using any instruments, neither were they available. We need more Pathani Samantas in Odisha, not cyber coolies who waste their formative years doing low end, data entry work in the name of IT. Institute of Life Sciences is working in oncology drug delivery systems which would revolutionise cancer treatment. The youngsters are bright, intelligent, and skilled but need direction. Our start up platform should coach them and not only be engaged in connecting them to government schemes, which even a smart website can do.

I find a deep connect between intellectualism and

statehood. Exercising intellect, putting it to use, would mean *thought investment* for the state. Undivided Ganjam, Mayurbhanj, Deogarh, Balasore, Sambalpur were fertile grounds for brilliant minds who had straddled across politics, literature, and science in the past and have given us this state. We are naturally gifted, peaceful by nature, blessed by divinity and possess a noble lineage. What stops us from thinking?

After all intellectualism is the only *ism* without any obdurate dogmas and hence is solidly sustainable.

Let us not squander it away.

"Mo Sarkar" in Odisha can be a global Model

'Integrity as wholeness and working together as one united Service' has turned around Singapore to a dynamo, though pocket sized. Rwanda is manifesting to be a global leader in change management. Rwanda Governance Board (RGB) is an autonomous body in Rwanda with a broad-based mandate to improve service delivery in the country and building partnerships that are crucial for the country's determined growth motive. Odisha with Mo Sarkar has the potential to recast the state to an economic juggernaut, emerge as a strategic powerhouse serving India's look east policy and playing a significant role in south Asia geopolitical equations.

Mo Sarkar could strengthen the state from 'inside'. It is change management – a drive to reform Odisha from a low-income economy to a high performance-high growth system for equitable socio-economic development. So, Mo Sarkar needs to be owned by the provider and the consumer equally – by the government and the people equally and on a Mission mode. The big dream of $1 trillion economy would not be an unassailable target.

By now it is certain that Gross Domestic Product (GDP) is less than adequate as a measure of the economic health and welfare of our societies. Alternatives like Gross National Income (GNI) are being expounded. Whatever the measure is, governance and growth are inseparable. Without improved governance, the economy of a state would flounder in spite of short-term capital infusions or trade incentives. Long term economic development is unfeasible without effective and efficient governing system. Introducing performance measurement systems in public services of the government is a mammoth and complex issue. Before it is imbibed into the system, the initiation is expected to generate some backlash and ire among the last mile service providers and the clients (the people or the citizens). With growing assertion of the clients (people), the public services would need to brace up to be more accountable and open to be accountable. This is going to change the face of bureaucracy in any state. Odisha has silently and without much hoopla has rolled out the 5T mantra of management. If implemented strategically and consistently, 5T has the potential to charge up and rejuvenate the entire state machinery like never before. Teamwork, Transparency, Time, technology & Transformation are the tenets to prepare the state to introduce and execute performance measurement systems which could place Odisha as the top contributor to national GDP. It can be done.

Odisha has launched a new governance initiative called 'Mo Sarkar' (literal English translation: My Government). This initiative took off at all police stations across the State along with 21 district headquarters hospitals and three government-run medical college hospitals at Cuttack, Berhampur and Sambalpur. The programme will be effective in all the 30 district headquarters hospitals of the by October 30. Health & Home (Police) departments would start making their services better, targeted oriented and consumer friendly. Because there is a feedback system built in and the monitoring and evaluation can be done by the higher ups randomly. The phone numbers of people who are coming to government offices will be collected, randomly with the purpose to improve the governance system by collecting feedback on behaviour and professionalism of government officers. The objective of the programme is to provide service with dignity (for both the provider and the beneficiary – the State and the People) to people who go to government offices with different grievances and needs. They should be meted out the 'best' services. I have worked in innovative governance programs in a few places and have noticed that lack of utilisation of government schemes hits the growth of the community and renders it less productive, downscaling by about 30%. What's the point in having government schemes when they do not reach the intended customers? Or they reach inefficiently or are offered unprofessionally.

'Mo Sarkar' if administered with the active participation of the Collectors, would transform the State like never before. Big ticket investments are flowing in and many are in the pipeline. Investment needs a basic core or a foundation to help it achieve triple bottom line. Odisha should exhort the investing corporates to work sustainably in the state. The three bottom lines or the three P's: people, planet, and profit have to be assured. With the auction of mines, growth in manufacturing, specifically in SME sector, implementation of the Kalia scheme to cover more than 16% of the population we need efficiency in governance.

The PRI (Panchayati Raj Institutions), Zilla Parishads, Panchayats should take the responsibility of driving Mo Sarkar with the help of the Police and Health. These institutions, thought themselves are clients, cannot absolve themselves from the task of assuring quality services. They are equally responsible. The Mo Sarkar drive should not result in 'passing on the buck'. To achieve 'ownership' of Mo Sarkar, the front-ending delivery personnel, departments and desks need to be trained, coached and handheld. Their capacities need to be enhanced with the help of the government training institutes, academic institutions and district authorities. How do you expect the line departments to align their own personnel on citizen satisfaction, performance score cards and feedback mechanism, which they have never been exposed to?

The HR implication of Mo Sarkar is the clinching factor. The feedback received directly from the customers (read people) will be used to rank employees in the order of their performances and those with good rankings will get out-of-turn promotion and action will be taken against employees with negative rankings. The performance-based reward system is hoped to sift the good from the deadwoods.

This sounds death knell for the poems (kabitas) and musicals which many of our officers, am told, churn out during office hours. Every paise of tax payer's money is accountable and the concomitant development it spurs has to be properly executed by the state machinery.

The responsibility of implementing Mo Sarkar, a gamechanger for Odisha, lies with the civil society too. The onerous task of sensitising citizens, mobilising their collective thoughts, assessing ground realities have to be undertaken by you and I. Officers need support in rolling out programmes, they need data, feedback and last mile help in management. Citizens need awareness of the schemes, their rights and responsibilities. Currently there is no 'third sector' which speaks to both. This third sector is the civil society.

Mo Sarkar can be a global 'good practice' which can showcase resilience of a small economy and the determination of a state to develop an 'answerable public system' despite formidable odds.

Growingly our societies should seal and are sealing space for freeloaders.

Perform or perish.

Migrant's Heart

The poem given below (in a set of three) depicts the emotional turmoil of a private security guard posted in a condominium in a city who in spite of the constantly morale-depleting poverty, remains romantic and free-willed. The poet has closely observed the life of a security guard who spends all his life shielding unknown people at the cost of his family and personal life. Is it 'abnormal' if he finds a little love in the condominium in his otherwise 'lovelorn and loveless' existence? This is the story of Biren, your migrant worker from Odisha, who doesn't know when he would go back to his family in his village and is completely unaware of what future holds for him and his folks. In between the uncertain future and the *grinding* past is the present where he finds his love, a beautiful girl in the condominium who hails from a family of "haves" in the condominium. Can he be in love? Can he express himself? Will he express himself? In the quandary, the Diva gets married to a person living in the block where Biren is posted now. That gives him the solace that she is back in his life, even if she is coming to someone else's house. Biren is sure that he would be close to her now and such is the dream of love in which he floats, albeit impractically. His heartless heart is happy even if all this is ephemeral. Even if his is a one-sided love, he is in cloud nine.

Poverty and heart need not be directly proportional and yet are always held against each other. Such is the animosity, and such is the strain pulling in opposite ways.

But Biren is happy. Let him be.

■

(1)
The Dart

This heart often prances around, even if asked to restrain,
When I saw her all ready, for a Saturday rendezvous,
Standing for her car, and our eyes met,
I had to salute her,
The best a security man can do,
Other than giving cover, sans the ability,
to keep own heart at abeyance.

She is my diva,
And I the security guard at her block,
With an existence in periphery,
A drifting life,
Moored for the moment,
In the condominium, where I found my love,
A love, which belongs to a world,
Of her and by her.

(2)
Cafune

How a small heart can lower the mind,
I was immune, till my peers relished,
Poking of the status, that trenched deeper to bury my heart
In the labyrinth of pettiness,
To shame my love, as love of the lunatic.
But lovers & lunatic need be the same,
Ain't they?
What is sanity, but the refuge of fettered pulses,
And my love is insane, unbridled.
The Diva & I,
Often, we meet in the park,
A little smile of co-existence, a little civility,
And how distance & proximity are the same,
For people sailing separate.
Last Saturday she came late,
With her partner & I had no rest,
Till I was convinced,
That with the lights, her body
Had also turned off.

No distance, however ruthless,
Can police envy, born out of love.
We met in the lift,
She drenched in perfume, I in sweat
And yet I *cafuned* her, telling her my story
My love & obstinacy.
Comes to a nought with the *thud* of the lift.
Here I am, grounded.

(3)
Proposal

Poverty & proposal are inimical,
I had the looks, but no books or hooks,
What Viji, my pal told me.
Proposal & possibility have to be together,
But why?
My mother still, is humiliated at the street corner,
The debt of food still haunts us,
My sister persists on a dream job,
The future has no promise,
My love still swaying to the last gust of cyclone,
Love & lovers are individuals, are different lives,
Ensconced in the 'game' of love.
My proposal is as short lived,
As my ever-changing posting, from one block to another,
I didn't see my Diva for days, and one morning,
She comes trudging in her trousseau, to a new life at my new block.
I know my proposal has worked & she has come to me,
Longer to my heart, maybe to some house,
But forever to me,
As long as I can dream,
Even with a heartless heart, Biren.

Odissi for the world

We have Lord Jagannath, the Lord of the Cosmos with us and everything emanates from Him and everything dissolves in Him. Every "thing" and every "nothing" is in Him.
Jatta chhaya lokamatra tribhubana janata badhate na tritap
Brahma Geeta
(Lord Jagannath shields the inhabitants in all the spheres or Lokas.)

So simple and non – complex are His ways that Jagannath 'belief' places the Lord as the friend of the devotee and as the 'walking, talking' Supreme. He participates in all human practices and habits and is the fountainhead of a stream of interpretation emphasizing the interior path, and of mystical devotion to God. A tradition in which He handholds humanity to ascend into the highest heavens and came face to face with God. Jagannath belief is the devotional interpretation of the soul's path to God, describing God as Love and not one which is scares or intimidates the devotee.

He is 'ଭକ୍ତର ଭଗବାନ'- Lord of the devotee. From ଦ୍ୱାରଫିଟା/ Dwarafita (Opening of the door) in the morning (in the presence of 5 sevayats, viz. Bhitarchu Mahapatra, Pratihari,

Muduli, Akhanda Mekap and Palia Mekap) to BadaShringara Dhoop & Khata Seja Lagi (bed time), Jagannath lives a day akin to typical humans. He is assimilated in His own creation. In this routine is included poetry, dance and eclectic entertainment.

At the slumber time, The Khuntia servitor recites Manima Daka Slokas and scatters flower petals on the beds of the deities. After doing so, he tosses petals up into the air to welcome all the divine beings who have come that evening to observe this ritual. The Lord is Surya Narayan while enjoying the divine slumber. The Sloka that the servitor recites is:

"Rajadhi Rajarajeshwer
Ishwara Thakur, Manima !
Anantakoti Brahmanda,
Ishwara Thakur, Manima!
Chaturdasha Bhubana
Ishwara Thakur, Manima !"... Manima Daka Sloka
("Oh Lord Jagannath!
You are King of kings!
You are Master of many universes!
You are the Controller of all creation!")

Before His sleep, music and dance was traditionally presented to the Lord which symbolised the cultural significance of the Jagannath 'belief' and the Lord's accent on music and various forms of art to 'cleanse' mortals and souls. Ratna Singhasana is believed to be the "Aum", the original sound of creation or the silence of sound. The music, dance and art forms outside the Ratna Singhasana are the different vibrations for the humans to move back into those vibrations and dissolve themselves to be one with the Universe. And that is the Oneness or the Advaita philosophy that represents Vedanta.

Odishan art forms, music, dance, and their diversity center around Lord Jagannath's belief, practices and philosophy. In Jagannath temple, the depiction of musical instruments such as Veena, Flute, Mardala, Dambaru, Kahali and Mrudanga indicate that these instruments were in regular use in the temple. The rulers of Ganga dynasty encouraged "Geeta Govinda" to be included as a part of the ceremonies of Lord Jagannath. As per the Madala Panji, Kabi Narasingha Dev (1282-1307 AD), the successor of Langula Narasingha Dev, the patron of the Konark Temple, introduced singing of "Geeta Govinda" accompanied with dance in the temple1. Hence along with music the "Mahari Dance" form was introduced in the temple. The Mahari dance form has been delightfully ritualistic and was dedicated to Lord Jagannath and performed by Devadasi dancers at the time of Badasinghar ritual during Lord Jagannath's bedtime. Identified by the Mahari dance, the Devdasi were also called as maharis which stands for mahanari or 'great lady'. Devadasi literally means 'female attendants of God'. Many believe that Rambha and Menaka can be considered the first devadasi to have danced for Lord Jagannath. The tradition of conducting seva or services of music and dance as part of the ritual worship of Jagannath is ancient. Nachuni or dancing girls have been part of the team of sevayats performing these services from the very beginning, and so are the mardalika or percussion players and kanatalika or cymbal players. The devadasis through the practice of mahari dance provided the earliest known platform for the development of culture of Odisha, driven by Jagannath faith and philosophy. The Mahari dance initiated the development of the world famous Odissi and the Gotipua dance forms of Odisha. These forms are among the biggest culture exports of Odisha to the world culture.

Devadasi in Odisha was often referred to as Radhadasi symbolising the highest degree of pure and selfless love towards Jagannath who is beilieved to be Lord Krishna in a different form. The dasi, by her submission, exercises proximity with Him. She was held in high esteem and were associated with auspiciousness and were supposed to be the embodiment of the charm to ward off the evil eye.

The dasi of the Lord was betrothed to the Lord and their union had all the characteristics of a marriage ritual as is traditionally performed in Odisha. The typical features included: exchange of garlands, tightening of the sari around the head, application of red powder and sandalwood paste on the girl's forehead, circumambulation of the temple. In the evening the young bride was taken to the palace of the Puri king by her mother and other female relatives as the king was venerated as the moving image of Lord Jagannath.

Immediately after the ceremonies, the training of the girl starts with lessons, imparted by her adoptive mother and her spiritual guru, mostly of devotional songs and the Puranas. She was also given lessons in dance. Her training continued for six or seven years or even longer while she lived a spartan life all along. The entire period was devoid of any ostentation and was always in the presence of the Lord. And the connect with the Lord was complete and absolute and bereft of any worldly interests or luxuries. She had the privilege of having her body, after death, covered with the same sari she received during her marriage with the Lord and having the embers for the cremation brought from the temple for her pyre.

The ritual services were divided among the Devdasis. Those who sang inside the garbagruha (sanctum sanctorum) at the time of Bada-Singhara dhupa (the Lord's dinner) were bhitara gayani. The second batch consisted of nachuni, who danced in the audience hall adjoining the sanctum sactorum, the patuari, who accompanied the deity in processions and danced on the road; and the bahara gayani, who sang outside the temple usually accompanying the deity in a procession. The bhitare gaani were considered superior and had the privilege of being with the Lord in His private apartments every night before he went to sleep. She sang from the Geeta Govinda depicting mostly the sringara rasa. She stopped only when there were signs of the Lord dozing off - such as drooping eyelids, or the garland offered to Him by His wife Laxmi beginning to fade. At this juncture, the voice of the singer herself would begin to fade away gradually. This is probably the exalted state of 'divine union – one where music joins the divine with the mortal. Odissi is born out of such higher manifestations of energies.

There was dance performed daily at the time of sakala dhupa or midday meal also. The midday meal usually started when, with the door of the sanctum still closed, the offering of the food began and it ended when the arati was performed after the completion of the meal. The duration of the dance depended on the length of the puja every day. The performance usually consisted of nritta (rhythmic dance), accompanied by the sound of the pakhawaj (percussive instrument) without any melody or song. Jagannath would have a clear, unhindered view of the dancer behind whom stood the Raj Guru with a golden cane, representing the royal authority. The dancer would, at the beginning, execute a triple turn to be able to offer a triple obeisance to both God and King. These nuances are present even in the contemporary styles in Odissi dance. And the devotees present would stand and watch from both the sides, almost like an atrium.

Acclaimed writers and devotees have described the dance performed during sakala dhupa as "...the dancer, one writer saw as a school boy in the very temple of Jagannath... about six or more decades back was supremely beautiful and gorgeous. She was fully Aryan in complexion with the lovely tan in the Puri balmy weather. She danced in absolute silence for about half an hour to the simple but exciting rhythm of a small pakhawaj played on by perhaps her Guru, an elderly man. The whole performance was a real piece of aesthetic dedication to the Lord... And after the dance was over, the writer was amazed to witness many devotees, young and old, men and women, rolling over the very ground that the young devadasi had danced on...". This sums up the holy and divine dance of the Devdasi and the ingenuity of Odissi dance form, which has flowed from the blessings of the Lord.

Even outside the temple, during the Chandan Yatra, Champaka dwadasi (three days before the full moon of the lunar month of Jyestha (May-June) when the marriage of Krishna and Rukmini is celebrated), hera Panchami and Rath Yatra, the Devdasi had significant role in performing arts at the divine precinct.

Sashimani Devi, the last Devadasi, died on March 19th, 2015 at the age of 92, and heartfelt obituaries poured in from international media (including an elaborate obituary in The Economist). Our media and intelligentsia were unexpectedly parsimonious.

A classical form of dance, music born out of divinity and marriage "made in heaven", Odissi is straight from sanctitude.

Art knows no spite. Promotion of exotic Odissi knows no respite.

■

CSR & Atmanirbhar Bharat

The practice of CSR is not new to the companies but there is an upsurge in the number of companies getting into the fold of CSR and the total CSR spend. If this increased spending under CSR is to achieve results on the ground, per its objectives, then it needs to be done strategically, systematically, and thoughtfully. Many companies till view CSR as charity or philanthropy. There are now professional managers handling CSR and their professionalism gets applauded if they can increase pressure to give CSR the character of a business discipline and demand that every initiative deliver business results. This is not CSR but business. The young CSR managers, who are actually managing on-the-ground CSR do not comprehend its main goal: to align a company's social and environmental activities with its business purpose and values. The companies must refocus their CSR activities on this fundamental goal of human development and provide a systematic process for bringing serious coherence and discipline to CSR strategies. Atmanirbhar Bharat provides them with the desired window to increase outreach and effectiveness.

The belief of "shared value" — creating economic value

and value for society concomitantly, is absent. There is no ingrained value system in the practising managers of the companies on CSR. Mostly CSR is a 'placating tool' for IR issues for greenfield industries and for others, good to be featured with. Most of the companies should be interested in totally integrating CSR with their business strategies and goals than in devising a cogent CSR program aligned with the company's purpose and values. And this has to be stitched together with the company's credo and motto.

Because now it is expected that CSR directly supports the Atmanirbhar Bharat initiative. The vision of Atmanirbhar Bharat would be achieved when each stakeholder in the larger socio- economic ecosystem of the nation e.g., corporations, academic and research institutions, civil society and the government can collectively contribute. Corporations play a major role because they have the resources, the professional manpower and the ability to create "development labs" in targeted areas. The COVID-19 pandemic and the territorial challenges faced on the borders have created a situation where it has become imperative for India to reduce dependencies on global supply chains, and focus on creating innovation and entrepreneurial ecosystems that would lead to economic and technological self-reliance and self-sufficiency through home-grown success stories. While these are possible, they would take some time, because they need to be comprehensive.

It is not only about encouraging start-ups and innovators, but there is a need to proactively engage with large corporations who own the best of talent and resources, especially those that are willing to partner with governments to achieve this vision. Corporate patriotism calls for prioritizing nation before profits. They can create niche products and services that have socio-economic benefits and make them available at affordable prices. There is a need to create a collaborative innovation ecosystem between the government, corporations, academic and research institutions. This is the development lab I mentioned above. Innovations need encouragement and the corporates are best suited to do this and provide a "buy-back guarantee" to the innovators and thereby securing the socio-economic stability of the innovator at the grassroots.

While many IT companies are acknowledged for pioneering India's IT revolution and also creating wealth for its stakeholders, it is lesser known that they have also contributed fine solutions for India's socio-economic wellbeing through research, development and innovation. Many are consistently engaged in creating an ecosystem to foster disruptive innovations for social and commercial purposes through the establishment of offshore development centers focused on research and design. This is an example of how industries can directly support Atmanirbhar Bharat.

Farmers need a lot of support under Atmanirbhar Bharat. An agro-advisory system for farmers needs to be in place actively. It would ideally provide services such as weather forecasts, pesticide, and fertiliser advisory. It should allow farmers to use ICT for solving farming challenges through personalized advice in their local language. For those using the service, field efficiencies should result in over 40% increase in yield, and over 10% reduction in pesticides and fertilizer usage (as per empirical assumptions and impact of a few fledgling programs underway a few years ago).

For long decades, each of these have been working in silos. Government institutions with huge budgets for social, defence and infrastructure sectors have depended on imported ideas, products and services thereby creating dependencies. Academic institutions produce fabulous research, which hasn't been translated into products and services of national interest, like how it has been done in many developed countries. Corporations that attempt to co-create products and services in collaboration with academia and research institutions, aren't sufficiently engaged with or their product/service used at scale to provide solutions to key challenges facing the nation. In this context, I'm highlighting the example of a corporate innovation ecosystem that I studied while writing my latest book.

While working towards an Atmanirbhar Bharat, governments will have to leverage disruptive socio-economic innovations and interventions in long-term national interests. This would not be possible in isolation but through collaborative execution with diverse stakeholders including corporations that have the best national talent and immense resources to experiment with ideas. Although many companies embrace some vision of CSR, they are hampered by poor coordination and a lack of logic connecting their various programs. The CSR programs buckle under the pressure of the district authorities who often act under various pressures. So, the CSR is seldom need based. It is pressure based. We can count the numbers of CEOs who are actually involved in CSR. Hardly a few. While working towards an Atmanirbhar Bharat, governments, including the local authorities, will have to leverage disruptive socio-economic innovations and interventions in long-term national interests. This would not be possible in isolation but through collaborative execution with diverse stakeholders including corporations that have the best national talent and immense resources to experiment with ideas.

Integrating business strategies with sustainability initiatives, successful companies allocate resources to ensure wellbeing of stakeholders which also enables the company to acquire a key differentiator vis-à-vis its competition, thereby making the business sustainable. GE's medical equipment division commits huge resources in African countries donating equipment to enhance healthcare to low income groups.

It is fine to comply with the mandatory provisions of the Companies Act. Nevertheless, CSR initiative driven by voluntary spirit is more intense and sustainable than that driven by the regulatory measures. For creating long-term impact and contributing to the developmental endeavour in the states, companies must integrate their CSR programmes with the schemes of the government. Partnership with civil society organizations and NGOs for planning and execution purposes is desirable. Every state must establish a CSR platform by the CSOs (Civil Society Organisations) to guide and institutionalize CSR programmes in the states. This may ensure more optimised management of CSR resources which will complement and supplement the state's development efforts. Almost half of the districts in India are off the mark to reduce the mortality rates of newborns and work towards the target under Sustainable Development Goal 3 for 2030. The target is " by 2030 ", end preventable deaths of newborns and children under 5 years of age, with all countries aiming to reduce neonatal mortality to at least as low as 12 per 1000 live births and under-5 mortality to at least as low as 25 per 1000 live births." India still has the world's highest number of deaths, about 1.1 million per year every year, among children under five and newborns, worse than sub-saharan Africa.

COVID has devastated our rural economy and lives. It is imminent that corporates suggest ways and means of partnering with the district or state authorities and implement livelihoods and skills programs for the youth.

There is so much more to do, and the companies and their CSR managers need to realise the significance of CSR in nation building, specifically under Atmanirbhar Bharat.

(Charudutta is the author of India's first CSR White paper)

The silence of the energy & the enigma

Ratna Singhasana (literally meaning bejewelled throne) is the lotus shaped rostrum at the innermost chamber of Puri Jagannath temple. This is also called Ratna Vedi (bejewelled platform) and is the seat of the Lord – the three deities Jagannath, Balabhadra & Subhadra who are accompanied by Shree Sudarshana, Shree Devi, Bhu Devi and Lord Madhava, making it "the Sapta vigrahas" or the seven deities. The chamber of the Lord is not a mere seat of resting but is believed to be the dynamic energy field of the universe from where the Supreme bestows blessings through diverse shapes, geometric patterns, 'blueprints' and 'reactors' – the divine energy sources. And this chamber of energy is also the 'zone of silence', the place of no-thought or *shunya*.

antar vedi maha punya vishnoh hridaya sannibha
(Skanda Purana, Utkala khanda)

The Skanda Purana in the fourth chapter mentions that the angels, the celestial bodies, the devatas (the Lords) love to be at Ratna Singhasana to pay obeisance to Lord

Jagannath & His company. Such is the magnetism of the Lord on the Ratna Singhasana.

The benediction from Ratna Singhasana reaches every soul, matter and place in the cosmos in utter and blissful silence. I have myself experienced an eternal silence inside the sanctum sanctorum. He is Silence.

aste yatra svayamdevomuktida purushottamam dhanyastevibudhipraksya yevasanti kulenarah,

In the place the Lord Himself, the Supreme identity and the most worship able figure, awards liberation to the very fortunate souls who live there under His protection."

bharate cot kaledese bhusvarge purushottamedaru rupi jagannatha bhaktanam abhaya pradah,

and protects His devotees from all fears."

The Lord is the epicentre and he rests at the navel of the Conch, the Sankha Khetra or the conch shaped location. The central area of Purushottama khetra is called Nilachala or Sankha khetra, described as a daksinavarta sankha (a special Lakshmi conch shell with the hollow part on the right side) having an area of 16 square km (the original area including the periphery) of which some part is submerged under the sea. The Lord being at the navel is meaningful.

This invisible energy, called Prana, is vital life force, which keeps us vibrant, healthy, and alive. The navel or the Manipura chakra functions as an Auric energy generator. Shakti in this chakra is Lakshmi and She is the goddess of spiritual prosperity and of wealth. This chakra through the power of Lord Karthikeya represents the power of youth. The Lord being at the navel of Sankha khetra which is the Ratna Singhasana bestows on humanity, the source of personal power and governs self-esteem, the base life energy, and the power of transformation for the Universe. The element of this Chakra is fire and the colour are yellow, bright like the sun. And hence the Beshas (the attire of the Lord) has colours which are in sync with the energy colours or nuances. The multi coloured appliques which are tied with the Kanka mundi over the deities on the Ratna Singhasana bear colours which are earth colours, and which radiate energies, unimaginable.

"The entire area of Orissa is full of holy places, but the city of Puri is the holiest of all." (Reference: Utkala Khanda, Skanda Purana3.52-3, 4.5-6).

The Utkala-khanda (1, Skanda Purana33-35) also mentions that "the land to the north of the seashore and to the south of the Maha Nadi ("the Great River") gives all other holy places in the world their powers. The land becomes holier with every step one takes southward from Bhubaneswar (Ekamra Forest) to the ocean. The land by the ocean, where the blue mountain (lauhala) stands, is the most secret of holy places, coveted even for Brahma.

And at the centre of the blue mountain the black granite Ratna Singhasana is placed in full regalia amidst the sanctum sanctorum which is 48 ft. high, and is a square hall of 30ft length and breadth. And Ratna Singhasana or the bejewelled throne is 4ft. high, 16ft. long and 13 ft. wide. Facing East, Ratna Singhasana has seven parts which are, Pindi, Kumbha bandhi, Kanthi,Alasha, Stambha, Kanaka mundai and Antargruhi. The deities are placed on the Pindi, which means platform in Odia and round shaped brass plates, called Nabagrahabaitha are fixed to the Kumbhandhi. Nabagrahabaitha and its relevance can be gauzed from the fact that the 'Graha (from Sanskrit gráha— seizing, laying hold of, holding is a 'cosmic influencer' on the living beings of mother Bhumidevi (Earth) and the Lord has the reins of these nine (naba graha) major influencers.

Grahas influence the auras (energy bodies) and minds of beings connected to the Earth. Each Graha carries a specific energy quality and the energies of the Grahas are getting connected in a specific way to the individual auras of humans. The nine planets are transmitters of universal, archetypal energy. The qualities of each planet help to maintain the overall balance of polarities in both the macrocosmic and the microcosmic universe - as above, so below. The planets, stars and other celestial bodies are the living energy entities which influence the other beings of the Universe and the Lord does the entire leela (play) from Ratna Singhasana.

The Vishnu Purana states:

hiranyareta samdiptam puranampurushottama sakalamnisk- alamsuddham nirgunam guna sasvatam

"Lord Purushottama is described in the Puranas as radiant as the Sun. He is all-pervading and transcendentally pure, simultaneously undivided and manifesting in innumerable forms, beyond all material qualities and the personification of all qualities."

There are many descriptions of the Ratna Singhasana, all manifesting towards it being the 'seed' of the Universe, the core. The core is always silent and hence Mahapurusha Vidya refers Ratna Singhasana as the Primordial sound, the Aum or the Pranava. Mmm, the humming sound of a bee, is the Pranava mantra. This is believed to be the sound of our Pranan or breathing. Therefore, it is called Pranava - the sound of breathing. And Pranava is the root mantra of Aum. The whole universe is created from "Aum." Souls are born on this earth, because God wants to release them from bondage. It is to "Aum" that souls owe their liberation. After the deluge, when the Lord again decides to create, "Aum" is heard. Thus, everything has its origin in

"Aum." Ratna Singhasana is the Mystical, Reverberating Sound Aum. The syllable Om has significance not only in Hinduism but in other religions and cultures, including Buddhism, Sikhism, Jainism, besides Indonesian and Nepalese cultures. Before Creation began, there was an empty void, which was then filled with the vibrations of the sound of Aum, believed to be a manifestation of the Supreme Lord. There is complete 'quietness' in Ratna Singhasana or Ratna Vedi and this is a unique situation where a throne or a seat of governance and primordial sound co-exist with the blessings of the Lord. This explains the 'justness' of the creation, the balance between root the flower.

akaranetradayas cha ukaraadharasthata
makaramalides- e chanadabindu prakatita
eshohi pranavakara purusha purushottama

"Jagannatha appears to be shaped in the form of Pranava (Aum): His eyes forming the letter A in Sanskrit, His lips form the letter U, His complete face forms the letter M, and His tilaka is the nada bindu (anusvara)."

(Reference: Mandukya Upanishad)

Amidst the 'surround' of silence and the absoluteness of Aum, Ratna Singhasana is the lotus. Verse 32 of chapter 9 of Mahapurusha Vidya describes Ratna Singhasana as the hundred petalled Lotus lapping the Saptavigraha (seven deities). It describes Lord Jagannath as a newly formed cloud – an imagination trying to unfold the beauty of a floating, heavenly benediction on earth. The Sapta vigrahas are Shree Jagannath, Shree Balabhadra, Devi Subhadra, Shree Sudarshana, Shree Devi, Bhu Devi and Lord Madhava. The deities of Bhu devi and Shree Devi are metallic (silver and gold respectively). Ratna Singhasana on a hundred-petalled lotus signifies Sahasrara or crown chakra which is considered the seventh primary chakra, according to most tantric yoga traditions. It is the most subtle chakra in the system and relates to pure consciousness. All other chakras steering this cosmos emerge out of this chakra and Lord Jagannath is the 'realisation' of Nirvikalpa Samâdhi. This stage is said to bring about rebirth or the siddhis - powers of transforming into the divine, and He urges humanity from the portals of Ratna Singhasana to attain divinity in speech, thought and action.

Covid -19 & Utkal Divas 2020

The world has shut down and everyone is home bound. On this Utkal Divas, Odisha Day on 1st April 2020, we need to join our souls, knit our families even stronger and resolve that we would do our best not to regress to the demeaning moniker of 'poor state'. We are no more a poor state and Odisha's Gross State Domestic Product (GSDP) has been projected to grow at 6.16% in FY20. This is significantly lower than the growth registered at 7.9 % in FY19. However, in the wake of COVID 19, FY20 & FY 21 are slated to see a steep fall in growth. FANI has hit our economy and so has the mining & metal industry slow down and the slump in manufacturing. It has been a bumpy ride since 16-17, when the growth was more than 15%. FANI in 2019 led to a crop loss estimated to be over 1.52 lakh hectares of land spread over 14 cyclone-hit districts. The rural economy is mostly dependent on the cultivation of crops, even today. The state's economy was devastated.

While we grapple with about 6% growth in Odisha now, the next 24 months look challenging due to the aftermath of COVID 19. Aftermath, because I assume that the spread of the virus would be arrested by June, which leaves only half a year to limp back to work. As I am writing this, there are more than 1.5 Lakh Odia migrant workers marooned in different parts of India. After 2 weeks, if the lockdown is de-clamped and work resumes at their locations then they would be able to take care of their sustenance, otherwise they would continue in a jobless situation for at least a quarter. If they return to Odisha, desperately and which is a natural instinct, they would again take about a quarter to get used to farming in their villages – either own farmland which they had abandoned or as agriculture workers. Because by June - July I wold not expect the mining, manufacturing and service sectors to bounce back to capacity engagement. They can't because their business is undoubtedly and inevitably connected to the global economy. China is fast resuming business but this doesn't mean that there wold be immediate resumption of goods and services to be exchanged between China and outside. Europe is so badly mauled that I don't foresee a full-fledged, celebratory Christmas for it this year. IMF has already said that each month's closure of the sectors is depleting about 3% GDP of Europe (average). If Germany's economy is expected to hit a bad recession and output going down by over 5%, one can imagine about the other countries.

My reading, amongst all these uncertainties (with no idea of when the virus war would abate) is that for an economy like Odisha it would result in a U-shaped recession curve that would begin in the last quarter of this calendar year with a bit of slower decline but then will remain at the bottom for an extended period of time, till about 18 months before turning around and moving higher again. I am still in the dark. I don't have answers to the basic questions - "When will it end?" and "How quickly will we recover?".

No one knows. We are fighting the deadliest battle of human history.

To arrest distress migration to other states, Odisha has planned a special livelihood package for four districts Bargarh, Bolangir, Nuapada and Kalahandi. The labourers would get increased wages under National Rural Employment Guarantee Act (NREGA) and loan from local self help groups at no interest rate. We need to create more work immediately after the virus abatement to rehabilitate the workers under MGNREGA. They are landless labourers and so we can't expect them to quickly sow their fields. Under the plan, the migrant labourers should get a daily wage of Rs 286.30 under NREGA instead of the earlier Rs 188 per day. They will also get an assured work 200 days in place of mandatory 100 workdays. Hence, there is a plan underway, hopefully, to design work creatively under MGNREGA and this should be expedited. If we don't engage labour then there is the bigger risk of moral bankruptcy across the state. The cost of labour for the real estate sector in places like Bhubaneswar, Cuttack, Berhampur, Puri, Sambalpur, Jharsuguda, Keonjhar and Rourkela would rise steeply. With petering out demand, the real estate sector would find it difficult to complete the projects. RERA should prepare itself with an early policy and economic readiness to handle this situation which is almost imminent. All eligible construction workers should be registered under Odisha Building & Other Construction Workers Welfare Board. It is planned to extend social security to them by providing them with marriage assistance, pension, education assistance and pucca houses along with other admissible benefits. But the time to do this has come. Without these systems in place, post COVID 19, the situation might run out of hand. District level MIS and Central data base at State level needs to work to track migrant workers and ensure linkage with welfare schemes. Today the linkages are weak. COVID 19, with everything frozen, would further deteriorate this. So, our online templates for working on the labour plans need not stop. The existing data on migration, for example, has not been saturated (data entry) so far. Without proper data records, no authority can help implement the schemes.

Our migrant population, engaged outside Odisha are mostly found in Mumbai, Andhra Pradesh, Chhattisgarh, Gujarat, Tamil Nadu and Telangana. Nearly three lakh people (last year the numbers were less due to local engagements) from western Odisha migrate to southern states due to drought (less rainfall in 18) and ensuing poverty. Much of Odisha's 7+% growth rate doesn't come from jobs – organised or unorganised. So MNREGA would be an immediate dose for resurrecting the rural economy after COVID 19 paralysis. The state should operationalise the corpus fund of Rs 500 crore (which is planned) so that the workers would be paid their wages in time. Outstanding under MNREGA, countrywide has been its undoing.

When industry, manufacturing, mines and services are left without business, we need to provide stand by to the rural economy through Livelihoods programs because Odisha today has a strong foundation of Self Help Groups (SHG) who get financial assistance from Community Investment Fund (CIF) and Vulnerability Reduction Fund (VRF). Any labourer in distress can avail the benefits of VRF but the state has to ensure that the labourers, who have lost everything are heard and their sufferings mitigated. Only then the schemes will be lively otherwise they remain good documents for libraries.

A famous phrase says that , 'the cure is worse than

the disease'? I don't think that it's just the coronavirus that kills people. This total economic shutdown will kill people." That's my paranoia.

According to the Odisha Economic Survey for 2019-20, the state's GSDP is performing at an average annual growth rate of 7.5 per cent, and this is a faster rate than the national average rate in the few years. But in this growth story, the contribution of industries sector has been about 40% , service sector about the same and agriculture is approximately 20%. Under the present circumstances it would be near impossible to provide the services sector any supporting infrastructure. Without that the expansion of services sector is impossible and so the potential to generate more engagement in in the formal sector will be minimal. This will have a direct impact on our youth force's employment opportunities. The tertiary education sector – the management and engineering colleges would face low demand or low placement. The state has to provide extra incentives to start ups and micro businesses to enable youths to eke out their living. Otherwise we could face a social upheaval, because we are talking about more than half of our population. NABARD, SBI and other PSU banks do always consider special drives but this time the other banks need to join the bandwagon. There should be instructions from the Finance Ministry. This could also help absorb the shock of decreased production, to some extent, in the manufacturing sector because there would be a worldwide sharp decline in demand. But a lot would depend on special packages, the easy bank interest rates, interest moratoriums, collateral management and staggered repayment facilities.

When we started in 1936 our financial state was painful. We received a grant of Rs 40.5 lakhs from the government of India and an additional non-recurrent grant of Rs 9.5 lakhs. Today the Gross State Domestic Product (GSDP) of Odisha is hovering around Rs 5,33,822 crore. We are one of the fastest growing economies in India, despite us being under Climate Emergency.

COVID 19 is also an emergency and we will emerge winners. Just that we need to plan out together, involve the civil society and give district-wise responsibilities to civil society organisations to work with the district governments in a more inclusive manner.

Many allied sectors like entertainment, hospitality & tourism would be in doldrums. They are in the danger of facing a negative growth rate. Social distancing would disable films, events, gatherings, travels and all kinds of social & group activity. Presently they are locked down.

Our strength lies in our agriculture sector including fisheries (though it has not developed desirably) which has always stood by us. Let's not neglect that.

Amidst global house arrest, Odisha might seem a dot but for me my state means my globe.

Vande Utkal Janani

Science of Internalisation

(Antarik = T+C+iP)

(Fireside chat on Atmanirbhar Bharat)

"Atmanirbhar Bharat, if implemented as envisioned, would change the *atma* of India, forever". A self-reliant India would not only build the capacity of the country but would engage all in the working age group and bring about a socio economic revolution in the country which not only the country but the entire Region has been aspiring for. Atmanirbhar would help make India's economy dominant and rekindle the social ethos." These were some of the thoughts expressed by Mr Charudutta Panigrahi, the Indian thinker and Futurist during a fireside chat with Mr Sandeep Behera, a communication expert and journalist.

During the talk Mr Panigrahi mentioned about 'woke capitalism" and how CSR would play a critical role in localising Atmanirbhar Bharat. After the recent amendments in CSR regulations in the country, the corporate is looking at the community programs with renewed vigour. From Reliance Jio's Made-in-India 5G plan to the recent boom in desi apps and PPE manufacturing,

Indian industry is preparing for a swadeshi turn and this journey has to start bottoms up. Quality supply is the clinching factor and that can happen when we inculcate the spirit of excellence in workmanship among the working age group from village upwards. The movement for 'Made-in-India', 'Made-for-India' and 'Made-for-the-World' products has to start from the ground and CSRs would have a major role to play in behaviour change, rural entrepreneurship and innovations. The scarcity in the availability of PPEs for management of Covid-19 positive cases prompted the garment manufacturers in Tiruppur who started making them in a small way. After learning the process of manufacturing these garments and getting their samples approved, at first only a few units started making these PPEs. But the orders kept coming in, the business expanded, pegged today at whopping Rs7000 Crore segment. What started as a completely humanitarian gesture turned to be a large business opportunity. Across the country, both large and small manufacturers, began to make PPEs. For a market that didn't exist three months ago, India is now believed to have become the world's second largest producer of PPE suits.

COVID and related lifestyle is the new norm. WITH new consumer needs after the lockdown, many companies saw an opportunity, where previously nothing much existed. Food delivery platforms turned into grocery suppliers to provide contactless purchases of essentials. Indian edutech firm like Byju's, are experiencing huge registrations in their app. Mr Panigrahi spoke about the concept of Antarik which is an equation (propounded by him stating a TED Talk) explaining the diffusion or the absorption of social schemes or reforms amongst the communities. He is of the opinion that any shake up in the availability of products and services in the country due to the embargo on imports can be met by the Indian manufacturers and developers provided we realise that there is Time, Communication and Participation (**Antarik = T+C+*i*P** (Time+ Communication+ *internalisation* Participation) which are crucial factors to change our economy as a whole. Another example of fast adaptability was due to the sudden opportunity which came when the Indian Government banned a number of Chinese-owned apps, most notably, TikTok. Overnight, an estimated 200 million users of TikTok in India were available as consumers. A number of new and old Indian apps have since tried to capture this market. Roposo, one such platform had already been growing rapidly reaching about 50 million users. Jio could soon create a super-app like China's super app WeChat where a user can do multiple things, from hailing a cab or making payments for purchases to chatting with friends and a host of other things without once exiting the app. The streaming platform Zee5 is also working towards becoming an Indian super-app.

Mr Panigrahi believes in the adage 'trade is good but imports are bad'. Atmanirbhar Bharat ('Self-reliant India') is the only path. Vital supply chains need to be kept within India. India's potentially huge domestic market should be tapped. He gives the example of *mittelstand*, the backbone of Germany's industrial wonder. Germany's small and medium-sized enterprises are the envy of the world and the backbone of the German economy. The country's "Mittelstand" companies, as they are known, include more global market leaders than any from any other country. The Mittelstand companies are strongly anchored in their region and have a strong connection with their employees and the local community. A similar foundation with SMEs can be laid in India with the help of CSR and not only CSR. In her announcements on the Atmanirbhar Bharat programme, our Finance Minister announced out a number of changes that redefined the scope of MSMEs. Output and productivity for Indian MSMEs have to be the drivers in the times ahead.

During the discussions, to a question of Mr Behera, he answered saying that 'we need to give business time to develop" under Atmanirbhar Bharat. Nothing happens magically. He elaborated on the following pointers:

- **Localisation of Atmanirbhar Bharat**
- **Sector analysis and demand forecast for MSMEs**
- **Skill gap analysis at the last mile**
- **Woke capitalism**
- **Antarik Model and how it can help reduce gestation period for MSMEs to provide goods and services to the home market without delay**

(In conversation during India International CSR Summit 2020)

Central University of Odisha
(Its uniqueness revisited on the 12th Foundation Day 2020)

The location of the Central University of Odisha (CUO) in Koraput brings to the fore the appropriateness of a knowledge hub in the middle of a paradox – a *tribal district*, with unparallel abundance of natural resources & an *aspirational district* trying to bridge perennial gaps in human development.

Koraput is the blessed land and the future of Asia. Blessed because from Lord Jagannath to fighter planes to Asia's mineral treasury, it is complete & the people are content. It is the sabar kshetra (the mystic land of the Lord) . This is the land where divinity and materialism co-exist in a unique balance. That is why the future of Asia – affluence of mine-able minerals, below the soil. Per capita income of Koraput should be one of the highest in India, but sadly always figures in the list of 'aspirational districts" of Niti Ayog. The reserve of 310 million tons in Panchpatmali mines is world's largest single-site bauxite deposit and yet Koraput suffers the indignity of infant death, large scale migration and rapid forest destruction. In Koraput 79% live below poverty line.

CUO as the knowledge hub would continue to play a direct role in shaping the human resources of the district, the state and the country. As a straight impact of a honed, better talented, specialised workforce will show in the human development of the district, the state and resulting Atmanirbhar (self-reliant) Bharat. The CUO's contribution in mainstreaming PVTGs and making them significant stakeholders in India's socio-economic growth story need not be underplayed. Mining royalty is the biggest non-tax contributor to the Odisha's revenue stream pegged at Rs 6130.97 crore from production of 270.84 million tonnes (mt) and supply of 287.80 mt minerals in 2017-18. The mining revenue is estimated to cross Rs 12,000 crore, 2021 onwards. Increasingly the local youths, educated and handheld by the University would join as skilled manpower in the industry and many can start their own enterprise.

In the last 12 years, which in local parlance is 1 yug (a significant time period representing the past, the present and the future), CUO has been able to aggregate the passion, creativity, and idealism of thinking minds, young and old alike, which have been applied to problem-solving and advancing our societal and economic well-being, not only in Koraput but in the country. The uniqueness of CUO lies in its strategic role in working towards localising SDGs (Sustainable Development Goals) in an *aspirational district*, an emerging state economy and a country aiming at a $5 Trillion economy in the next decade. The global Goals for Sustainable Development are consequently integrated into higher education and the practice of engaging students in these efforts, through projects and community interventions result in directly impacting our performance in SDGs. Because CUO is amidst one of the most primitive tribal communities of the world. An improvement in the development indicators here would bring about a quantum jump in all round performance on human development indices.

The CUO has taken futuristic steps in orienting itself to proactive nation building. Some of them are as follows:

· Aligning university governance structures and operational policies with the aims of attaining the SDGs

· Identifying and addressing any key gap in the university in a response to the SDGs

· Mapping how high-level university strategies, policies, plans and reporting indicators align with the SDGs

· Identifying organizational units and streams which are relevant to specific SDGs

India and Odisha specifically is experiencing climate emergency, large scale displacements due to COVID pandemic and increasing pressure of gainful engagement of the burgeoning youth population (more than half of the population is below 35). CUO is taking unprecedented steps to embrace its cultural, socioeconomic and physical setting. It is imperative that CUO be socially embedded, thereby fostering development through direct engagement with its immediate communities, which are low-income and marginalised. CUO is working creatively, take out-of-the-box strides to become a regional knowledge and innovations hub and a greater force of societal transformation. Universities must focus on the individual. It is fostering student success, steadily, by becoming student-centric – rather than faculty-centric. This is by enhancing its capability of being nimble, anticipatory, imaginative and reactive. The departments, the faculty members and the eco-system at the CUO is providing unique environments that prepare students to be "master thinkers" able to grasp a wide array of skills and information. It is encouraging to know that CUO is attempting to prepare the most adaptable workforce to meet the demands of the market, the economy and the country's requirements.

In the coming years, the University is slated to become an effective partner in the national & global development. Through the proliferation of networks between like-minded alliances, community partnerships through students and faculties can transformation occur at the scale that is immediately needed in order to advance our present state and national knowledge economy. Our communities including all of us, should target this imminent future and transform their thinking to see CUO, not as self-indulgent "people factories," but as valuable idea generator and implementor. Under the ambit of the NEP 2020 and the Atmanirbhar Bharat plans of India, CUO has the potential to wield influence and to manifest technologies and concepts that can change lives like never before, during COVID or post COVID or climate emergencies or any other impending disruptions. Innovation and adaptation, as ushered in by NEP 2020 are needed now more than ever before in our higher education infrastructure and in our development institutions of global effect.

Contemporary universities like CUO have a responsibility to transcend traditional disciplinary limitations in pursuit of intellectual fusion with vocational blend and develop a culture of knowledge entrepreneurship. CUO must be prepared to further delivering higher education at scale – in a manner that bestows status upon CUO based upon the outcomes it achieves and its depth & breadth of impact rather than the exclusivity and quality of their incoming freshman class, alumni or confines of a prescribed format only.

The uniquely placed CUO has the responsibility of transforming the socio-economic situation of the indigenous people (PVTGs), influence the academic enterprise of the high energy, young country and supplement the emerging status of Odisha as the nation's growth driver.

From Sunabeda to WEF (World Economic Forum), I see a high quality, high energy growth trajectory of CUO's participation in comprehensive development of all of us. CUO should evolve as the window to the world. Only then we can redefine mainstream and re-evaluate its uniqueness to mine more uniqueness.

It is our responsibility to ensure that CUO grows further as a place of light, of liberty, and of learning.

■

The companies need to internalise CSR

The practice of CSR is not new to the companies but there is an upsurge in the number of companies getting into the fold of CSR and the total CSR spend. If this increased spending under CSR is to achieve results on the ground, per its objectives, then it needs to be done strategically, systematically, and thoughtfully. Many companies till view CSR as charity or philanthropy. There are now professional managers handling CSR and there professionalism gets applauded if they can increase pressure to give CSR the character of a business discipline and demand that every initiative deliver business results. This is not CSR but business. The young CSR managers, who are actually managing on-the-ground CSR do not comprehend its main goal: to align a company's social and environmental activities with its business purpose and values. The companies must refocus their CSR activities on this fundamental goal of human development and provide a systematic process for bringing serious coherence and discipline to CSR strategies.

The belief of "shared value" — creating economic value and value for society concomitantly, is absent. There is no ingrained value system in the practising managers of the companies on CSR. Mostly CSR is a 'placating tool' for IR issues for greenfield industries and for others, good to be featured with. Most of the companies should be interested in totally integrating CSR with their business strategies and goals than in devising a cogent CSR program aligned with the company's purpose and values. And this has to be stitched together with the company's credo and motto.

Although many companies embrace some vision of CSR, they are hampered by poor coordination and a lack of logic connecting their various programs. The CSR programs buckle under the pressure of the district authorities who often act under various pressures. So the CSR is seldom need based. It is pressure based. Although numerous surveys have touted the increased involvement of CEOs in CSR, we have found that CSR programs are often initiated and run in an uncoordinated way by a variety of internal managers, frequently without the active engagement of the CEO. We can count the numbers of CEOs who are actually involved in CSR. Hardly a few.

CSR in India offers tremendous scope to create 'Development Lab' in the district and sub-district levels to help work systematically towards meeting the targets as laid out in the SDGs. The labs in turn can be replicated and can be truly supplementing the state efforts in development. Though substantial amount of CSR funds is invested, programmes are implemented without conducting need assessment in terms of geographic area as well as thematic sector. It would be worthwhile to put on the ground, a CSR Watch with the active participation of the industry, civil society, government, community, and the academia. CSR Watch could mainstream CSR further, at the grassroots and assist the districts with better planning for need based, targeted interventions yielding measurable results.

Even today, as I write, many corporate managements take CSR work as any other contract work and hence bracketing their NGO partners as "Vendors". There should be an initiative to clarify that NGOs are non-profit making social organisations and work at the community levels. There is no 'commercial business involved in their work and hence should be accorded 'equal' partnership rather than being relegated to being vendors supplying goods and services. NGOs often felt that this lack of understanding interferes with the social license to operate for the businesses, specifically in the extraction industry. Furthermore, there needs to be virulent advocacy for lifting of GST on NGO work. Non-profits or NGOs are not working for furtherance of business and hence ideally non-profits should not be covered under GST.

The early years of corporate philanthropy included contributions mostly in setting up schools, hospitals, community development, women empowerment, planting trees, nurturing art and culture. We were used to such noble gestures and 'feel good' initiatives, but these 'give-aways' were remotely connected with their core business. So, these initiatives get unsustainable, and can happen only till the point the company is profitable; more importantly, these 'largesse' by themselves will not drive the company to remain profitable or community centric. What is required is seamless integration of business strategy and sustainability initiatives. As an example, Hindustan Unilever (HUL) invests in research working with nutrition and health specialists in its 'ready to eat' food business trying to reduce salt to the recommended dietary levels, reduce trans-fat from vegetable oil, sugar from ready to drink teas, and drastically cut calories in children's ice creams.

Integrating business strategies with sustainability initiatives, successful companies allocate resources to ensure wellbeing of stakeholders which also enables the company to acquire a key differentiator vis-à-vis its competition, thereby making the business sustainable. GE's medical equipment division commits huge resources in African countries donating equipment to enhance healthcare to low income groups.

It is fine to comply with the mandatory provisions of the Companies Act. Nevertheless, CSR initiative driven by voluntary spirit is more intense and sustainable than that driven by the regulatory measures. For creating long-term impact and contributing to the developmental endeavour in the states, companies must integrate their CSR programmes with the schemes of the government. Partnership with civil society organizations and NGOs for planning and execution purposes is desirable. Every state must establish a CSR platform by the CSOs (Civil Society Organisations) to guide and institutionalize CSR programmes in the states. This may ensure more optimised management of CSR resources which will complement and supplement the state's development efforts. Almost half of the districts in India are off the mark to reduce the mortality rates of newborns and work towards the target under Sustainable Development Goal 3 for 2030. The target is " by 2030 ", end preventable deaths of newborns and children under 5 years of age, with all countries aiming to reduce neonatal mortality to at least as low as 12 per 1000 live births and under-5 mortality to at least as low as 25 per 1000 live births." India still has the world's highest number of deaths, about 1.1 million per year every year, among children under five and newborns, worse than sub-saharan Africa.

How can we grow when you and I , a citizen & a

corporate of this country, can't take care of the new born and protect a life? Corporate programs should look for integrations with government schemes.

COVID has devastated our rural economy and lives. It is imminent that corporates suggest ways and means of partnering with the district or state authorities and implement livelihoods and skills programs for the youth.

There is so much more to do, and the companies and their CSR managers need to realise the significance of CSR in nation building.

(Charudutta is author of India's first CSR White paper)

Late Sri Pramod Panigrahi

Father & father figure

On this day, 19th May my father, Sri Pramod Panigrahi, had left me, six years ago, bodily. Since then he has been with me, even closer. The more I observe myself, the more I realise that my genome, inherited from my parents, has been dominantly shaping my personality, more than the environment. I am sure yours would also be a similar case, but it is quite rare that we pause, introspect, and connect to our genes. On this anniversary I mull over the inextricable chord I had with my father and sense its ever-expanding influence. Studies suggest that gestures, language, reaction to incidents & people, thinking process, looks, body language, habits, feelings, and a lot more are constructed or copied from the genes. There are identified genetic links between psychological factors, established by scientists and which are known as 'the big five' personality traits. The broad sets are i) sociability ii) moodiness iii) agreeableness, iv) conscientiousness, and v) openness to experience. During the nascent, growing up years, when Nana (I called him that) took my maths or the English lessons, I was a bit awed because he knew everything. People around him swooned over him, his writing skills, his official notes, communication, and all-encompassing capabilities. Even in early years, instead of developing a complex, I always observed him from a distance and did my best to internalise him and not emulate because I couldn't. In my case I have probably forced the genes to play in me and not wait for natural draw, when it came. Even during his last days, I never stopped watching him, touching his feet in a light brush not to disturb his drug induced sleep, as much as I could. Some where I knew that he was also a father figure to me and was never a helicopter father. Fathering me came so natural to him and I consider that a benediction for me. During my choppy teenage years, or my early adulthood times, he shared music, literature, movies, folk stories from districts of Odisha with me instead of policing me or nit-picking. So confident was he of his genes that he was never in a jiffy to establish himself and never gave me any reason to be in extremes. This space for my growth lent me the invaluable, unfathomable, rock solid framework of life – between the rights and the wrongs. Now, in all these years, when my peers and acquaintances realise my quietness in a group talk, my fingers reach out to my Lord, my silent eyes get misty. What a wonderful nostalgia !

Nana himself knew happiness and was sensitive, and that is why he was able to feel for the child, and his feelings. Given to a lot of abstraction since childhood, my parents were my only refuge. I didn't have to wander around in the unknown environ to look for answers in those impressionable years. Genes never means a famous surname or a treasure of riches or the arrogance of hereditary success or feudalism. It is the constant trickle of learnings from one generation to the other, of the baton changing hands in a relay race, with the aim to usher in the man or woman of the future. Genes command our social behaviour, and the conjoint future.

The father figure that Nana was, opened my vistas and the world of possibilities - to books, authors & their lives, personalities, happenings, sartorial options, with no bias or pedantry. My choice of career was never parents'-dictated or driven by peer examples or complexes. I was never expected to nurture the killer instinct. Now I comprehend what independence means for human growth and potential. I am living a life, maybe with a fraction of his aptness but with the guarantee of his genes.

One needs a father and a father figure, ideally in the same person to bring in the fusion of hard skills and soft skills in a growing human being – the hands on and the hand off. Only then 'the child can be the father of man'.

The hero of Parinam (1961 film) Sri Pramod Panigrahi, the lyricist, the writer, the thinker, the jurist, the erudite, the aesthete and life partner of my Bau, our absorbing evening talks then perk up my life every moment now. At Swargadwar, I bowed to you and whispered, "my hero, thou shall live on, in my every heartbeat, in every fall and every stall".

You had once written to me, "you don't inherit genes, you earn genes".

It is work in progress, perennially.

(On the 7th death anniversary of Sri Pramod Panigrahi)

Gram Sabha & India's future

*T*he *Constitution of India under Article 243(b) signifies the Gram Sabha as the grassroots-level of village council formalised as primary, local self-governance system in India.* Gram is the unit of development and Gram Sabha is the enabler. I believe that *"Na Lok Sabha, Na Rajya Sabha, Sabse Upar Gram Sabha'.* It is meant to be that. *A Gram Sabha, translated as 'village council' is the only grassroots-level of village council that has a Sarpanch (Leader) as its elected head. There are about 250,000 Gram Sabhas in India. The Gram Sabha can influence decisions taken by the State Govt. Authorities and can influence & modify weak decisions relating to Agriculture, Animal Husbandry, Social Welfare, Health and Sanitation, within each Gram Sabha.*

The entire development process should start from the consent of the villagers in a formal congregation that possesses decision making powers. This parliament of the village needs to maintain a quorum - at least 1/3rd shall be women and the number of SC/ST participants shall bear the same proportion to the quorum as the population of SCs / STs bears to the total population of the Village Panchayat. From 500 to 1000 population of a village panchayat the quorum ranges from 50 to 300. The provisions made for the Gram Sabha in India is effective, practical and potent. Record keeping of the Gram Sabha is mandatory which includes attendance and proceedings. Keeping audio visual record is mandatory for the conduct of Grama Sabhas. There are many low income, backward areas where the gram sabhas have held sway over the decisions to allow investors in industry or mining companies and others to enter the geographies. The villagers have to decide about their own future and here comes the 'capacity of villagers' syndrome. In the name of building capacities many 'outside agencies/NGOs' try to influence the villagers negatively or with motivated interests. The compass of the villagers can be expanded legitimately and with positive reinforcement through a Master trainer/Champion program. A group of locals to take charge of preparing the rest of their co-villagers to take decisions for the good of the village. The Grama Sabha as a forum is expected to conduct Social Audit of all schemes pre and post implementation in the villages. Truly laying development in the hands of people. The onus is on the people to maintain the dignity, power and influence of the Gram Sabha. The South-eastern State of Odisha as a leading state of India, in mineral industrialisation and has had a remarkably strong growth of Gram Sabhas in different districts and more in tribal areas. If power dose not flow to the last mile, last house and last person, power holds no meaning. It becomes a bundle of waste not handled properly by a fistful of people with the perennial scare like that of radioactive substance, which doesn't differentiate between people and creation. Decentralization through Gram Sabha is a strategy to empower citizens to control their own destinies and to be specific fiscal measures. This signals that citizen collectives can come together to make decisions of allocation and expenditure of public resources. 'Democratic decentralization', as practised in India, is where this power is devolved to elected local governments—this was the spirit of the 73rd and 74th amendments to the Constitution in 1992-93.

A few years ago, citizens had no role in the development channels of even their own communities. In the democratic decentralization system, gram sabhas have been envisaged and treated as key platforms for popular participation.

Let's explain you how and what have been the impact of Gram Sabhas in rural India.

(NGOs meeting with the villagers)

Indigenous people occupy 22% of India's geographical terrain and constitute over 23% of the state's population. India's south-eastern State Odisha is a gifted land in the world because it has a mix of all – the natives who are rich with mineral resources, the unique art and crafts of skilled people with unbelievable piety and unparallel soft skills and invaluable land mass to foster rapid industrial growth (480 kms coast, large numbers of water bodies, reasonably higher ground water table, over 310 sunny days yearly, increasing forest cover) and trouble free labour force. The long coastline contains Asia's second largest eco-system of mangroves and some of the world's richest biodiversity. We are aiming at making the Metro Cities as skill capitals of India and ideally rural youths should be employed there. But industrialisation has to be rapid. The perennial question – can we or should we abandon the globally unique and superabundant flora and fauna and run the rat race towards destruction, pollution and contamination.

We would not have worried about industrialisation, if we knew how to tackle development along with clean environment, if we knew how to enforce ecological discipline among the companies playing with natural and mineral resources, if we knew how to respect the PVTGs, if we knew how to handle exploitation of land, labour and faith. Because rural region should not, at any cost lose its pristine wealth, its blessed existence and the benediction. The woodland of rural economic growth, tribality is the profound underline. It's all about tribals, from the Lord to the Mining, but they are the most deprived, utterly neglected and severely cornered.

Rural India is the treasure house. For example the State of Odisha in India has wealth - large reserves of bauxite (65%), china-clay, chromite (98.3%), coal (27%), dolomite (20.7%), fireclay, graphite (76.67%), gemstones, iron ore (26%), limestone, manganese ore (31.7%), mineral sand, nickel ore (95.1%), pyrophyllite, diamond and quartz. The stack of other minerals includes copper ore, lead ore, titanium bearing veneniferous magnetite, talc/ soap stone and high magnesia igneous rocks. Odisha possesses almost all of India's chromite, graphite, nickel, bauxite, high quality coal iron ore, beach sand. Yet the contribution of Odisha to national GDP is unconvincingly low. Sometime ago the economy of this State was equivalent to Ethiopia on nominal basis and equivalent to Ecuador on PPP basis.

Gram Sabha of indigenous community

The Rural India is starting to grow more dependent on service and industry sector and less on agriculture. A recent study the state faces 'acute' food insecurity due to a drastic decline in the production growth rate of major crops. The inter-district productivity gap is also widening. There are scientific predictions that Climate emergency is feared to wreak havoc in the coming years in States like Odisha, which would further debilitate lives, families and village economies. We also believe that fast economic growth, business potential and industry-friendly policy can make States like Odisha, a $1 trillion economy by 2030. India is expected to become a $10 trillion economy by 2035, and Rural Sector contribution is expected to be major. After Maharashtra and Tamil Nadu, economically poor States like Odisha could be the third State, by then to be a $1 trillion economy.

What is the role of the Civil Society?

So far the role of the civil society has been queasy and limited. We are aware that investment-friendly policies, good governance, robust infrastructure, mineral resources and agriculture resources and access to the market can make rural sector a complete development destination. But it all starts with the opening of the lock at the community. We are talking of development of the States and do we forget that development means 'of the people, by the people and for the people'. In this discourse of development, the only word scarcely used is 'People'. Only a Gram Sabha reminds us of the rights of the people to decide about themselves. But who works towards sensitising the communities who constitute the Gram Sabha? Where are the Civil Society Organisations, the NGOs? On one hand we have activists promoting their ISMs in the name of being pro poor and on the other hand we have CSR programs of industries engaged in tokenism in the name of development. Gram Sabha is the only key to development, bottoms up.

The mineral industry, specifically, depends on the indigenous rights and the development process, the principle of free, prior and informed consent (FPIC) derived from indigenous peoples' right to self-determination and their right to property through ownership or traditional use. How do the PVTGs in rural sectors know, what is good for them and not good for them before they take a decision? They should be informed and not mis-informed either by the industry or by the NGOs. At stake here is a reserve of

310 million tons, Panchpatmali mines, which is considered to be the world's largest single-site bauxite deposit. How many discussions have been organised with the local communities on this? How many of us know about the global ramifications of this process?

It seems that for the expansion project of large Govt Industries, Gram Sabhas are being organised by the district administration in villages. The villagers, while putting forth their demands, favourably and unfavourably, voiced parameters to support the company to carry out mining and developmental activities. But do the villagers know, what to ask for and what is their need? Is there any NGO or organisation there, to assist them assess their needs?

For the existing bauxite mines in rural segments, a Public Sector Industry has been awarded the highest 5-Star Rating of Government of India, for its sustainable mining practices and environment protection measures. Do the affected or involved villagers know what this rating means? What is their inclusion in the development process of rural sector? Have they been at least taken on a trip to show around how and what the company has done to adopt reclamation and rehabilitation processes for ecological restoration of the mined-out area? Is the area being systematically backfilled with lateritic overburden to form benches, terraces and leave-depressed area at strategic places to form reservoirs/ rainwater harvesting structures to support vegetation and wildlife. None of the villagers are aware of the process or the ensuing benefits of the processes.

Before the Gram Sabha sits, the people of the villages should know whether the Mine void has been reclaimed and afforested with trees of native species, having capacity to endure water stress and climatic extremes. Any company's genuine efforts for environment protection also need to be disseminated amongst the direct affected people and not confined to the preserves of intellectual presentations in state capital and country capital.

This because Gram Sabha is where the action lies. It is the council holding the key to the development of the country. If State like Odisha is the gold mine and the global repository, then Gram Sabha is the door to the treasure. More so, when we are discussing rental economy.

An Aluminium Industry, with all its seemingly precautionary measures and pre-emptive steps to conserve nature and recharge water, had to face opposition at the second Gram Sabha, held at the panchayat office for its bauxite mining. The locals feel that the local economy and household wellbeing of over 5,000 people of four panchayats depends on rural hills and on minor forest produces. The local people use the stream water of the hills for agricultural activities. They are of the opinion that when mining starts, the streams will go dry and their economy will collapse. Who is there to spend time with the Rural Gram Sabhas, which is spearheading the anti-mining movement and share

legitimate data, information and case studies to sensitise them? Their reaction should be genuine and fact based, not political. The Civil Society has been under-performed in deep dive, long standing community intensive work. Can you name NGOs which work sustained with the community, notwithstanding external funds support? Taking CSR contracts for limited period of time is business of development, not Social development.

Gram Sabha in Rural Districts:-

Gram Sabha is probably our last, coveted democratic tool, working bottoms up. It would play a decisive role in charting a course for the future development of India. Gram Sabha would allow;

· India getting on to the fast lane of development

· Rural segments discarding its poverty tag and take on the high growth, 'Smart' development brand

· The transition of natives from a forest-based dwelling to more mainstreaming, while maintaining equity and ecology

· The trade off between reckless expansion (in the name of development) and real development in lives

Our last bastion of aboriginal simplicity and naivety should not be corrupted with manipulative systems which would rob them off their soil. This whole fight for international wealth making is for their soil.

Let's all develop. Let's all prosper. But legitimately.

Gram Sabha would script our future growth story. Nurture, empower & respect it.

The *verandas* of Kala Bhoomi

Odisha always deserved a spiffy crafts museum and Kala Bhoomi is the one. Spacious and breezy, the infrastructure is smartly designed to showcase the typical Odia social infrastructure with an 'agana' (courtyard), tulasi chauraha (tulsi plant kept in the courtyard and revered), a baula tree or a neem tree in the middle of the courtyard and the walls coloured in mud/clay colour (light brown) with brown tiles roofing. The entire ensemble is in brown, different shades of brown. What is striking is the combination of verandas and the courtyards.

Each section of the museum opens up to a wide, spartan veranda. The stretch of the veranda mirrors the pan of the open mindedness of the Odia craftsmen. Odisha craft has unique character – subtle and yet colourful, distinct and yet inclusive. The saree motifs, the tribal metal implements, the stonework, as examples, are delicately designed. Kala Bhoomi, literally translated to Craft Land in English is unparallel in the eastern part of India and is among the top bracket in India.

Museum is not a place to horde or stash crafts. It is a crucial tour down the legacy route. It is almost like revisiting the family album. Kala Bhoomi transported me to the 'nostalgia of last mile creativity' in Odisha. Where all this had begun or begins. The genesis of Odia identity. A visit to Kala Bhoomi should be a permanent fixture for school students and college students, from all over the state and outside too. The management of Kala Bhoomi should use ICTs (Information & Communication Technologies) to showcase the centre in social media to reach to the younger population. I remember going to Nandan Kanan on school trips which were exciting and educative. Kala Bhoomi has a café which can cater to the crowds and make the outing interesting. The café can be a good hangout. I have not seen Kala Bhoomi during functions, but it is an ideal place to hold crafts related gigs, events, workshops, residencies, talks and soirees. Networking with the embassies of countries like France, Austria, Japan, US, UK, Indonesia, would be beneficial to the entire art community of Odisha and India.

Presentation of crafts is important than the population of crafts, is what I believe in. It is not only the number of artefacts or the collection which is important but also the way they are spread. Kala Bhoomi has used space rationally with scope for further expansion, if need be. That shows.

Odisha craft has strong Regional symbiosis and the influence of South Asian motifs, hues, characters is well known and warrants detailed display and propagation. There cannot be a more appropriate platform than Kala Bhoomi to do this. Space could be dedicated to a R&D centre inside Kala Bhoomi where the students/artists could spend time researching, learning and promoting the 'international connect' of Odia craft. This could be a specialised residency program. This would add the contemporary global vein to Odia dexterity. Odisha needs to promote art & crafts in a rehashed style. More futuristic. Kala Bhoomi has the panache to take us back to the future. The bandwidth needs to be built. The civil society organisations of Odisha should lend hand to the management of Kala Bhoomi. In many ways Kala Bhoomi can contribute to the 'Look East' policy of the governments.

I am not talking about the collection and display at the centre because this would keep changing keeping in view the thematic changes, trends, the variety, the produces etc. But having such a dedicated, modern centre for art and crafts is in itself an achievement.

It is our responsibility to strengthen the centre, its outreach and its effectiveness. For the verandas of Kala Bhoomi would be the new space for Odia aesthetics to flower. Verandas open mind spaces, and verandas breed comity, the epicentre of Odisha's soft power.

After all 'danda pinda', terraces and 'baranda' (from veranda in English) is the Odia ground zero.

The stone at Kala Bhoomi, so appropriately tells you that 'the soul of India shines through the skilful hands of Odisha."

So true.

Silence of Civil Society

From a basket case to a trillion-dollar economic powerhouse. Odisha appears to be set for the big leap. With a steady growth rate averaging upward of eight per cent, the state is likely to beat several other developed counterparts in the country before the next five years and touch the trillion-dollar mark by 2030. In fact, Odisha would be one of the major engines of national growth, which targets to touch $5 trillion by 2024.

But at what cost?

Sometime ago, much more than 50,000 trees were felled at Talabira village, less than 20 km away from Jharsuguda, which is fast emerging as a prominent industrial zone of India. These trees were cut to clear forest land for an opencast coal mining project, jointly developed by Neyveli Lignite Corporation (NLC) and the Adani group.

As always, the promoters of the coal mines are prepared with all legal formalities whereas the villagers, though custodians of the entire 1,038.187 hectares of forest land, have no titles under the Forest Rights Act (FRA), 2006. They would be hapless witness to the massive felling of over 1,30,721 trees. On March 28 this year, the Union

Ministry of Environment, Forest and Climate Change gave Stage II clearance to divert 1,038.187 hectares of forest land for the coal mines.

The civil society in the region is curiously indifferent to this large-scale devastation.

It was imperative for the office of the Chief Conservator of Forest, Sambalpur to call for a meeting with the local civil society organisations and village committees to inform them about the upcoming mining activities and take their views before this kind of a step. But it was not considered necessary. Is the Forest department meant for protecting forests or destroying them? This is a cruel paradox.

This is particularly worrisome as Odisha is on the verge of a climate emergency and such steps need to be carefully planned with the help of environment specialists. The latter, which include NGOs, some of whom are winner of awards for their stellar work, have not let out a whimper of protest. They should learn a few things about protection and conservation from forest-dwellers.

The entire forest patch has been traditionally protected and conserved by the forest dwellers at six villages, including Talabira. They have an organisation called Talabira Gramya Jungle Committee which has the social mandate to conserve and guard the forest. From their meagre means, they had appointed a guard. They paid his family three kilograms of rice.

They have protected the Talabira forest for more than half a century, with the innocuous belief that the forests 'belonged to them'. More than 3,650 people are dependent on this forest. But how would they know that the whole conspiracy is so well crafted that everything would be labelled under 'development' and that everyone was in cahoots against them. This is where the civil society should have been intervened and turned vocal.

The forest-dwellers lack legal recognition of their rights over the forest. The FRA rules, 2012, necessitates that the forest officials concerned help raise awareness about the Act and its provisions so that any future claims and the processing thereof could be done in a more social and humane manner.

The move for clearing forest land for mining activities should have taken into consideration the local sentiments. It has failed to take cognisance of or of any recognition of the people's rights. Though there is a provision under FRA for the officials to create awareness among people, there has been no communication whatsoever with the locals. Forget awareness.

According to a July 30, 2009 circular of the ministry, Gram Sabha's consent has to be acquired before diversion of forest land for other usage. I have been writing about the issue of open violation of FRA and non-compliance with an MoEF circular on July 30, 2009 during diversion of forest land for non-forest purposes in the state. Why is gram sabha avoided? It is probable that their consent is forged. Ironically, since 2008-09, the Sambalpur and Jharsuguda forest departments have been allocated Rs 74 lakh and Rs 14 lakh for FRA implementation.

I am reiterating that EIAs (environment impact assessment) should be prepared by independent consultants and not by project cronies/advisors and that there should be strict punishment for fraudulent public hearings and all public hearings should be video-graphed by an independent agency.

The governments at the Centre and state had recent discussions on the production at Mahanadi Coalfields Ltd

(MCL), land issues and law and order problems at the coal site and it was decided that the glitches would be solved in 15 days. But it seems what was not discussed was the possible investigation of auction of Talabira coal mines which has an estimated deposit of 554 million tonnes (MT) with an annual production capacity of 20 MT. This coal will feed NLC's planned 3,200-megawatt (MW) Talabira Thermal Power project in Odisha and the company's 1,000-megawatt (MW) coal-based project at Tuticorin (Tamil Nadu). The total compensation of Rs 1,200 crore is planned to be made to the families affected by the Talabira-II & III coal blocks where Adani Enterprises is the mine developer-cum-operator (MDO).

Many of the civil society organisations working in the state, and the Sambalpur area in particular, are aware of the issues with mining in the region but have chosen to look the other way. Their silence at can have a devastating impact on the people and ecology.

Samuel Sahu (Babi)

Samuel Sir passed away, this day in 2000. He was an actor's actor. If Odia acting had a school, he was the shining star alumnus. Present day actors, anchors are unfortunate because many can't retrieve his films or theatre plays because Odia film has no documentation or archive. Zilch. Some may have a few retro recordings saved with their families or acquaintances, providentially. An indefatigable, improvisational genius, Babi babu straddled the worlds of Odia theatre, radio drama and cinema with a baritone, sophistication and confident diction unknown till him. On every occasion where I have to mention about spoken Odia language and diction, he is my quintessential example and inspiration. His dialogue delivery was amazingly natural during a filmy era where it was mostly melodramatic and lengthy. He bucked the trend and heralded conversational style. Listen to Akhil Mohan Patnaik's radio drama adaptation *Ruby ra Rubai* where he gives voice to the character of the betrayed husband, a train driver, from Jatni. He befits the story – both the writer and the actor, ahead of their times. Manik Jodi, Adina Megha, Kie Kahara, Bhai Bhai, Sadhana presented some of his sterling performances. In 1940, after quitting steady engineer's job at Chakradharpur, he joined Kabichandra Kalicharan Patnaik's New Odissa Theatres (which revolutionalised Odia Theatre) and over a period of time he directed and acted in over 200 plays in his log association with Annapurna Theatres too. A career change, quitting a stable engineer's job for a life with uncertainties in Odia entertainment industry speaks of his passion and the encouraging ecosystem available in Odisha, then. Odisha was culturally vibrant and had an appetite for erudition. Sri Jagannath in 1949 was his debut in celluloid. Babi Babu has been awarded with Guru Kelucharan Mohapatra Award, Odisha State Film Award, Sangeet Natak Akademi Award, Jayadev Award.

His simple lifestyle was unbelievably unassuming. He lived near my school. The Gentleman of Odia screen, he was the darling of the Odia audience because he was the genteel, suave hero or the big brother(bada bhai) who was conscientious and unflinchingly sacrificing. He exuded the responsibility of carrying the family tradition and legacy on his shoulders. Babi Babu was class and yet could easily reach out to the mass because he made their idol visible in front of them. He spoke Odia the way it is meant to be and was the family head, the way Odia joint families were knit together. His measured acting, terrific screen movements and plain speak dialogues erased any differences between real and the reel. He was there with you, talking to you. In Odia acting if true life persona ever influenced performance status and vice versa, it was in the case of Babi Babu. Rarely ever after.

Balraj Sahni and ilk remind so much of him.

The art of destroying Bhubaneswar

My moral apathy and selfish bewilderment have destroyed the idyllic Bhubaneswar. My self-claim of piety in the city of Temples, is a cunning repose of escaping my responsibilities as a citizen and validating my freeloading on the government (nee, a sponge). If it suits me, I am an advocate of the government and if it does not then an on-the-spot critique. Governments, whether state or national, are the easy target, the whipping boy. The efforts for making it a Smart City or the Global Sports Hub are government initiatives. The civil society has no role to play in any aspect of the life of Bhubaneswar because there is no civil society. No one assists the government in the policies, initiatives, or the implementations. Everyone is waiting for an invite from the governments to join as an Advisor. This invite and tag are crucial because of the perks likely to come associated. If not invited, then I have nothing to do with the city or the public planning. I am only a consumer – I know how to consume and not care.

Population-wise Bhubaneswar at about 11, 69,000 counts among the world's 500 cities. It started as a town of government colonies but it now Headquarters India's natural resources business, is a Hub of global sports, an Education Centre of India, an emerging axis of international tourism. It still continues to be the biggest settlement for Odias from all the districts of Odisha and rooted NROs. Almost all the public servants who retire, settle in Bhubaneswar and the number of residents directly connected (or formerly connected) should be in the range of 26-27000. They know the system, they can influence their co-Bhubaneswariyas, can find solutions to many day-to-day city life problems, can motivate youngsters to pioneer self-service, encourage many youngsters who are currently exploring technology solutions to civic issues and above all can earn recognition for themselves. At least for the lure of recognition.

The state population is 4.37 Crore. In the next 15 years, it is expected that over 17 percent of the population would be in cities (or city bound), out of which Bhubaneswar is estimated to attract over 80 percent of this migration. The city is already bursting at its seams now. By 2030, Bhubaneswar would house the stakeholders of the great India growth story because it will be the capital of the capital. Odisha, the projected steel & metals capital of India would be the principal provider to India's targeted 300mt steel capacity by 2030. Due to Odisha's bountiful resources, all the world trade houses would flock to Bhubaneswar. This growth story would be written in stories, literally – now there is no cap on the height and floors of high-rises in the capital. The buildings can be more than 27 metres tall and can have 23 floors and more, whether residential or commercial. BDA has so far given permission to 108 multi-storeyed buildings in the city. Are we aware of this development? Or are we still floating in the poetry of 6th Century and the relics of Odisha's south east trade? I need not be a philistine but in the same vein I need not be a dilettante. Even the art & craft need my sincere involvement, not lip sympathy or tokenism.

To support any infrastructural plan in Odisha, IIT Kharagpur gives the seal and that seals the fate of all our responses and reactions. Our planners say that "In order to meet the housing requirements, we have no other way but to give permission to multi-storeyed complexes". Because the unassailable IIT Kharagpur says that there would be a shortage of nearly 4.5 lakh dwelling units by 2030. But in all these assessments & decisions where is the civil society of Bhubaneswar involved? The moot question is "where is the civil society"?

I am the ostrich that buries its head in the sand. Being a crab and an ostrich is not an enviable combination.

Bhubaneswar is the knowledge hub of India, supposedly – with all kinds of research, educational and professional institutions actively running their businesses. Had any of them participated in this study by IIT Kharagpur? Did they ever show any interest? Are the teachers or the students or the research scholars aware of the developments in the skyline of the city? By 2030, when Bhubaneswar would be reeling under climate emergency (further supported by wanton constructions), I am sure they would be still holding classes and selling admissions. Because admissions matter. Even when Bhubaneswar falls under seismic zone and is the Centrepoint of climate disasters, I develop a strange apathy. Bhubaneswar might need to grow vertically, so be it. But do the people of Bhubaneswar decide about Bhubaneswar? No. There is no individual effort nor is there a community glue. It's all discursive, fragmented and consciousness in smithereens.

My complacency could be a case study. The other cohort I find comfortable is that of activism. Enough of that. The shortest route to headlines is government criticism and reviling. I have an estimate of how activism and its trade has increased the poverty levels of our state. I have watched over the years, how activism spurs a business model that thrives on schadenfreude. But that is a different disquisition.

Immediately as COVID tapers off, the city of Bhubaneswar would be dug up. With the start of the construction work migrant labourers would rush to the city from different districts of Odisha and neighbouring states. Slums would multiply in the city in the next 3-4 years and by 2035-2040, the slums would have to be gradually regularised. The support service would become expensive, all the residential areas would be swamped with high rise apartments, in place of small houses of mostly retired government servants and old families. Crores would cloud nostalgia, change the city's innate character while a whole generation (of present youngsters) would be outside. When they come back and if they come back, they would be foreigners.

Is this the ultimate fate of Smart Bhubaneswar and Splendid Odisha?

Bhubaneswar is a blessed city with a terrain which can help design it like a hill city. But it is late. The skyscrapers can be confined to a particular part of the city and not poke their heads unpleasantly in every corner. Bhubaneswar overall can be kept low rise. The commercial area can be separated from the residential areas. This one move could make Bhubaneswar much cleaner, overnight.

We need a Smart City as an urban space that is liveable and ecology-friendly, technologically integrated and meticulously planned with the use of information technology. Bhubaneswar is the much-coveted destination in India, where the rush to the city is more evident than ever before and it has been duly accorded the smart city status (in the first lot of 98 cities) by the government.

Some of the residential projects have blatantly and arrogantly violated land acquisition in the past and have build their properties right on top of natural stream and aquifers in the city. They are the sector experts who preach socio economic development on chat shows. I hope they would soon learn to be entrepreneurs and not businessmen only. There is a big difference.

Till date, as I am writing this, there is not a single Bhubaneswar Citizen Forum in the city. The city, the seat of power and pelf, has scores of retired Babus, technocrats, wealthy traders, power brokers who I always assumed, were competent, influential and powerful. But that was an illusion. Not only are they incapacitated but are pathetically short sighted. They are in some stratosphere, wallowing in their own antiquated CVs, hallucinating about some glorious past and rattling medieval literature and demoded *kabitas*. Antediluvian shenanigans. The youngsters are preparing to leave Bhubaneswar at the earliest. By 2030, the common language in Bhubaneswar would cease to be Odia.

Let's think for ourselves and shake ourselves off from this paralysis. It is the responsibility of the civil society to help the governments. The governments would ideally want to be 'less of government and more of governance'. But how will they be? The civil society is not civil. It's apathy for Bhubaneswar smacks of a weird dislike and loathing for one's own place.

This is the Temple City and is also the Knowledge City. The silent, coy, reticent city, Bhubaneswar is probably the only city in India to have this alchemy. There is an eclectic mix of divinity and modernity in the city. Why am I so short sighted? Why can't I help the governments to help us? Why am I so dependent on the government for everything? Why don't I take responsibilities and stop passing on the buck? That is because I am the self-destructive Bhubaneswariya, who probably doesn't deserve the wonder city.

The true cost of all the complacency is the death of the soul.

By 2030, not only the landscape, water table, human development but the soul of the city would have evaporated. The temples would probably be the only witnesses if they are allowed to survive despite the lure of their real estate worth.

Here "Nero" is not fiddling, he is lecturing on Ashoka for the 2023rd time.

In the meantime, Daya river has ceased.

Please do not kill Bhubaneswar !

Theatre in Odisha

Anant Mahapatra is the renaissance Man of Odia Theatre. 2019 onwards he is Dr Anant Mahapatra with an honorary doctorate conferred on him by Ravenshaw University, his alma mater. In India, awards probably indicate swansongs, but in Dr Mahapatra we find a livewire charging up every moment to innovate the theatre space in Odisha. He breathes drama. In the last six decades and more he has seen it all but not done it all, because his appetite is insatiable. New lighting techniques, subtitling of dialogues for non-Odia audience and adapting international storytelling is a routine experiment in his "Purabi" lab in Bhubaneswar. Odia theatre from its birth has been routinely experimenting notwithstanding severe financial constraints. That's the madness of the medium for Odia and Odisha. He and Odia theatre have travelled together for almost six decades now – co-habitating. From leftist inspired college platforms to present day tech-driven, device dominant presentations, he has been an active witness to the changing times of India and Odisha going through waves of changes – cataclysmic changes. From IPTA to WhatsApp, he is omnipresent and omniscient.

From the era of government patronage to corporate endorsement, he is equally at home with his craft. Central to his life is his craft and not icons. He is an iconoclast.

When many would choose to thrive on government funding, he openly miffed with his peers for diluting the craft for doles by philistine upstarts. Hailing from a privileged background, he chose the less chartered journey of a whole, long life of Drama. The gumption and steadfastness show even today. Many term it as obstinacy. Whatever, but it comes with uncompromising quality, ruthless discipline - not even in a little misstep on the stage and minor blemish on the makeup. Perfection is absolute for him. It is said that Ramshankar Ray, the maker of the first play of the Odia theatre, Kanchi-Kaveri, in 1881, was such a martinet. Dr Mahaptara has reengineered the craft many times over after the early pioneers of Odia theatre which included stalwarts like Bhikari Charan Patnaik, Kampal Mishra, and Godavarish Mishra. While theatre was gradually making inroads into Odisha, permanent stages for Odia theatre were erected by famous theatre aficionados of Odisha - Bira Bikram Dev's Bikram Theatre at Khariar and Padmanav Rangalay at Paralakhemundi.

Constantly inventive, Dr Mahapatra even advocates for dialogue-less plays.

Why do you need sound when silence speaks?

"He who does not understand your silence will probably not understand your words. ...

He laments the deliberately created crassness of the medium of Theatre to shake the box office. But he also ponders that power is always in democracy and in numbers. Jatra, the new blockbuster version of Theatre is tongue-in-cheek, street smart avatar of theatre. Theatre of the masses. True to the fibre of a creative soul, he accepts contradictions without an iota of ego or remorse. Even if sometimes these are the opposing forces in life which affects art directly. Because he is an existential thinker and craftsman. An artiste who has immersed himself in both cinema and stage theatre, shaped by his early life exposure to education in Cuttack and Allahabad and an enviable lineage.

In Odisha Jatra is an industry now with a turnover exceeding 120 Cr. These are moving troupes with 100-150 members including actors, directors, dancers, sound and costume assistants, lights men, cooks, technicians and labourers. This is an entourage like the erstwhile circus groups. The Jatra troupes spend almost a whole year travelling and are the common man's theatre. Odisha was not new to opera style of presentations – long dialogues, musical interludes, satires thrown in between but Jatra became the sleek, blockbuster opera with social subjects.

Theatre in Odisha took off at the same time when Odisha became a state – 1936. I find a strong link between the recognition of Odia language and its expression in theatres. Though limited to mostly the elites, Annapurna theatre was the first organised alma mater of stage performance and the Eton of Odia culture and entertainment. In 1933, Somnath Das formed Jayadurga Natya Mandali an opera party in Khandualkote village in the then Puri district. And in 1935 the opera party was revamped as a theatre. The tribe of artists grew rapidly and in 1936, the full-fledged Annapurna Theatre kicked off as a touring troupe. In 1933 the movement started in Puri and later Cuttack became the epicentre of opera party turned theatre style entertainment. There were stand alone, smaller theatre troupes like the Banamali Art Theatre but when a more institutionalised theatre group like the Annapurna took shape, the artists came flocking. The floodgates opened.

Traditionally Odias are artistic and culturally inclined – in different forms – art, dance, craftwork, singing, drama, music. About 8 decades ago, the encouragement and state support for art and artists was almost non-existent, barring the ones patronised by the royals. That too was limited in Odisha.

In 1936, Odisha created its identity as a political state and that was when the cultural renaissance also gained currency. It's about periods in the life of a state which become turning points in the lives of the people of the state too. This was the time when Utkal Sammilani spearheaded the Odisha formation agenda. The Odisha delegation, headed by Maharaja Krushna Chandra Gajapati reached London to negotiate with the British government. The group of leading Odias included the Rajasaheb of Khallikote, Mr. Lingaraj Panigrahi, Mr. Bhubanananda Das and Shyam Sundar Das. With the persuasion of the delegation, a report was published on behalf of the joint select committee which was accepted by the British Parliament. On 1st April 1936 Odisha became a separate Province after about three decades of tireless struggle. With tumultuous political scenario in the background, the culture brigade provided the outlet for creativity in Odisha which had no showcasing till then, in a professional and commercial set up. But success was yet to come till 1939 when Kartik Kumar Ghose ran a play (adaptation from a Bengali story and play) which was produced by Annapurna Theatre. It was successful in the box office and Its success ensured more support for theatre in a state not known for magnanimous support to theatre, art or music. Of course, I would still like to believe that the permanent stage patronised by Jaga Mohan Lala in Mahanga village, Cuttack district, was the first stage in 1875 and it gave birth to contemporary Odia theatre. Lala was a theatre buff and he wrote the first Odia social drama, Babaji i.e. "The Holy Man".

Odia theatre is very similar to tiatr in Goa which is over a century in age and it is the homegrown form of theatre that blends drama, comedy, tragedy and music, has been a crucial part of Goan life all these decades. In Goa, tiatr is staged almost 365 days of the year, sometimes twice a day. But traditional opera in Odisha revolved majorly around mythology.

After Kartik Ghosh's show, gradually the number of artists increased and then it was decided to divide the theatre company into two divisions and run from two places, Puri & Cuttack. They were run from permanent stages, unheard of then. The Annapurna A-group was in Puri and was managed by Bauri Bandhu Mohanty. The Annapurna B-group was in Cuttack. Ramchandra Mishra's Social Play, Manager, was probably the first big success in 1945 at Cuttack. Over a period of time the two groups A & B split and almost became competitors. But Cuttack, due to its prominence had a much better audience and commercial success than Puri. Annapurna at Cuttack had its own permanent stage at Tinkonia Bagicha. This iconic Theatre building is now grazed to the ground and has given way to a shopping mall. The revenue model for Puri division of Annapurna theatre was slightly different as they banked on touring. The viewership only in Puri was less and not viable to run a permanent set up. There was also a splinter group Annapurna-C which existed for a short period.

Odisha theatre then was greatly influenced by the Calcutta theatre. So was the film industry and the music. Indian People's Theatre Association (IPTA), formed in 1942 had major inroads into the stage and music style in Odisha. Some of the members of the group like, Bijon Bhattacharya,

Balraj Sahni, Ritwik Ghatak, Utpal Dutt, Khwaja Ahmad Abbas, Salil Chowdhury, Pandit Ravi Shankar, Jyotirindra Moitra, Niranjan Singh Maan, S. Tera Singh Chan, Jagdish Faryadi, Khalili Faryadi, Rajendra Raghuvanshi Safdar Mir, Hasan Premani, etc were connected in one way or the other with Odisha. Many of them including Utpal Dutt, Uttam Kumar, Salil Chowdhury, Gulzar, Girish Karnad, Mohan Agashe, Lilette Dubey, Mahesh Dattani, are personal friends of Anant Mahapatra. But seldom would you hear him flaunting. This speaks of his comity. One of the significant dramas supported by IPTA was Nabanna (Harvest). This Bengali drama, written by Bijon Bhattacharya and directed by Sombhu Mitra, portrayed the evils of the Bengal famine of 1943 and the alleged indifference of the British rulers and the ruling class of India, towards the plight of the millions of famine-stricken poor. The adaptation was a runaway hit. Though in Cuttack, Annapurna Theatre was a melting pot – artists from all over the state took to acting due to the platform. Artists from Ganjam, Koraput, Mayurbhanj, Sambalpur were actively engaged in different departments.

Art to sustain, needs professional management and a strong revenue plan. Both were lacking and both the Annapurnas - A & B were fast becoming losing propositions. Financially the theatres were languishing till they virtually closed in 1970, when they were struggling to run five or six plays annually. It was painful because Annapurna Theatre was the only organised theatre in the state, and they helped create a strong tradition in drama and produced brilliant performers, playwrights, and other stage personalities. They enjoyed a special privilege in cinema later, due to their grounding and experience in theatres. They were considered the masters of their art. In any case theatres, even today are considered the foundations for acting. Dramatists like Ramchandra Mishra, Bhanja Kishore Patnaik, Kamal Lochan Mohanty, and Bijay Mishra were products of Annapurna. But many untiring enthusiasts tried to keep Annapurna B running and breathe life into the cradle of Odia theatre. However, the final curtains on Annapurna Theatres came down in mid 1980s and abandoned thereafter. Such is the callousness that the mascot of Cuttack city and the state theatre has collapsed, and the infrastructure grazed to the ground. Annapurna has been the breeding ground or the nursery for actors. Noted cine and stage artiste of yesteryear Bhanumati Devi who passed away recently was born in Myanmar. She came to Puri and started acting on stage, Annapurna, before joining Odia cinema in 1954. She was an integral part of Annapurna Theatre, Cuttack, for about four decades. She has acted in Mrinal Sen's National Award-winning Odia film 'Matira Manisha'. From actors, such as Bhanumati Devi, Durlabh Chandra Singh, Nityanada Das to Dukhiram Swain to the founder gurus of Odissi, Pankaj Charan Das, Debaprasad Das and Kelucharan Mohapatra — Annapurna has been the foundation school of the legendary artistes of the state. But even after the vanquishing of Annapurna, Dr Anant Mahapatra, undeterred staged shows, trained new blood and experimented dauntless. Commerce has never scared him and will never ever.

Annapurna gave us pristine Odia performances (the acting, the diction, the storytelling, the powerful portrait of social issues) from icons and actors like Samuel Sahu (Babi), Hemant Das and many more.

Despite producing acting legends and entertainment doyens, Annapurna has frittered away due to gross apathy towards the state's theatre legacy. The Annapurna A in Puri and the Annapurna B in Cuttack have been struggling for survival. And after Phailin, the weak structures of the theatres have been reduced to ruins. The Annapurna in Puri was set up with the help of the then king of Keonjhar on a land that belongs to the Jagannath temple of Puri, which was a part of Uttarparswa Matha. Over the years, the troupe faced demise. Puri used to stage at least one play a month with the help of the local amateur troupes. But after Phailin, most of the structure had collapsed. Because of a litigation over the land in a case between the matha and the Jagannath temple administration in the Orissa High Court, nothing can be done to repair and renovate the building.

In spite of its uniqueness and quality, the theatre movement with Annapurna couldn't attract young talents to keep it going. The Annapurna at Cuttack, formed in 1942-43 by Lingaraj Nanda was very popular in Odisha but couldn't survive. The infrastructure is dilapidated, and the leaseholders of the land have converted the land usage to more commercially viable business projects. Since the theatre complex has ownership in the name of a private person, the government is making efforts in going for an amicable settlement with the owner for renovation of the theatre. This apart, adequate step are planned to be taken to rehabilitate the old and retired artists living in the complex, If the government doesn't take focussed steps to revive drama and play culture in Odisha, then who would and who can? The Odisha government has committed to revive the two units of 'Annapurna theatre' established at Puri and Cuttack at an estimated cost of over Rs.10 crores.

We go on creating new platforms without taking care of the existing ones. The Annapurna theatres could never move with the times. The younger generations were never interested not did they know much about the theatres in

Odisha. Recently it has been encouraging to see trained youngsters doing excellent theatre work in Odisha. In October2006 a group had staged a marathon of plays stretching over eight-and-a-half hours. The event included six plays, each of 80 to 90 minutes' duration played with the intention of reviving the theatre interest.

This was the result of an emotional outburst of stage aficionados when they saw the collapse of the massive gates of Annapurna Theatre's arched gate way in February 2006 but how long can anyone keep squatters away?

Stage needs regular patronising both by the government and the people. Anant Mahapatra set up the Utkal Rangmanch Trust (URT) in 1997 with the pioneering and innovative idea of popularizing and encouraging professional theatre in Odisha and staged plays on a weekly basis. Quite averse to dependency on government funding, in 2005, URT presented "Women Directors Special Festival' plays from SAARC countries. The renaissance Man of Odia Theatre is one among the culturati. Over a century of plays staged in different states of India and his travel to many countries since 1958 has established his school of theatre, though not formally. Today we have brilliant young theatre artistes and enthusiasts who could gain immensely from Anant Mahapatra's experience, repertoire and depth. It's time we realise that we have a gold mine amongst us. Chittaranjan Tripathy, Biswaranjan Kanungo of Sunabeda, Surya Mohanty, Dolagovind Rath, are brilliant Theatre all-rounders of national calibre should utilise the mentorship of Anant Mahapatra. Anant babu has also been a jury member in several editions of the India International Film Festival and Indian Panorama and a member of state and Central Academies for several years.

While the legendary Kali Charan Patnaik the promoter of a company Orissa Theatre was the trendsetter in corporatizing Theatre in 1942, headquartered at Banka Bazar, Cuttack. He was the first to change the trend – from mythological to social plays. Govinda Chandra Surdeo, Mohansundar Deva Goswami, Ramchandra Mishra, Bhanja Kishore Patnaik, Gopal Chhotray, Ananda Sankar Das, and Kamal Lochan Mohanty are the other theatre greats of Odisha. Anant Mahapatra symbolises unflinching trust in the medium in a low developing state like Odisha, which has always been condemned to play second fiddle to theatre hotbeds like Kolkata, Mumbai or Kerala. Anant gave Odisha theatre the national stature. Never one to drop names of his celebrity friends, he is yet to be overwhelmed or awed. He is still hungrily looking for the extraordinary.

There aren't many business houses who could take art and culture as their corporate social responsibility in Odisha. We need to encourage contributions to art and culture. That needs to be developed as a culture and norm in the state. A state with the much discussed, soft skills of the people.

The unique feature of Odisha theatre is its resilience in the face of acute poverty and despondency. Creativity in the middle of helplessness, limited viewership, resource-constrained obsolete technologies, limping film industry unable to support theatre, unorganised art promotion and almost apathetic governments is unimaginable. Kerala, Maharashtra, Bengal have not lived through this. In Odisha art is the greatest survivor. If art is God then God has not given up in Odisha. Theatre artists had to take up jobs for their livelihood. Dr Mahapatra has braved the storm throughout.

Odia theatre in its centenary deserves a bow. Rise and

salute Odia theatre. It continues to act when the world around it is even inert.

The exceptional life of Anant Mahapatra is intertwined with the life curve of Odisha theatre. Both have loved each other, lived together and grown together. Someone called Dr Anant Mahapatra (I am sure he would not like the Dr prefix) is permanently betrothed to Odisha Theatre.

Long live the lovers.

Long live Odisha Theatre

Social distancing & Khatti

What are you saying? What social distance? ଆଜି ଖଟି ଯାଇହବନି ? କିଏ ମନା କରିଦେବ ? ଆମକୁ ଅଟକାଇ ଦେବ ? ଥାଉ ମ...

But when social media was fermenting in-person social distance, Corona accentuated it. For along time to come, there would be an inherent fear driving social bonding. That would be a terrifying impact of corona. Morbidity due to proximity is going to send communities around the world a different signal. Be careful of meeting people. I think that's a much bigger malaise.

We are fast turning to zombies. No naturality, but all externally commanded. The social quarantining could spur reclusiveness among youngsters. More youngsters because that's where the action has been and that's where the action is going to end. A whole generation would withdraw into individual, little shells. Would that mean that there would less of intellectual sharing, probably not. But what is certain is that there would be even smaller cubicles of interactions – whether in office or home or social.

You would have noticed that in the last few decades, broad based, macro thinking has given more to fact based, micro thinking. That's because we value everything in life in terms of investment. So if we are perennially driven by investments, we would always look for evidence for everything. And evidence would drive us to facts and figures. But the entire space of free thinking is gradually shrinking.

I have seen a lot of khati in places I had not expected - Greece, Spain, Estonia. Small group of men (mostly men) milling around a street corner and spending time aimlessly or leisurely, without any haste. Remarkable is the way people find out time and newness every time they meet the same set of people and in similar social and physical settings, day in and day out. This is an ode to the human spirit, which is always craving for intimacy despite close proximity. Maybe that intimacy can't be saturated? Or it cannot overwhelm.

I think the closest to Khati in English language would be a commune. If Lagom in Sweden signifies balanced living or knowing limitations in our everyday life "Not too little. Not too much. Just right.", then Hygge in Denmark philosophy denotes 'coziness of the soul', and Fika, the significance of taking regular breaks during work. But Khatti is a blend of all of the philosophies with it being more of a social construct, rather than an individual one. Khatti is more comprehensive as a philosophy and practice, much more than any. But as always, we don't value what we have and pine for what is not.

So, in Khatti you have action and inaction. You have 'social' and 'individual' and you have no stress at all. It is a resort, round the corner in Odisha. It is our export to the world under severe stress, always. Khati is about no stress, never.

So, when the FM radio screams 'hum corona ko harayengay', we should say , zaroor harayengay, kyunki hamarey paas Khatti hai".

Sociologists have discovered two distinct patterns in communes. Richard Sosis and Eric Bressler had studied 19th-Century communes in the U.S. The first feature was that more demanding communes lasted longer. Bigger sacrifices fostered greater emotional commitment to the group. In Cuttack, Berhampur, Bhubaneswar, Sambalpur and in many other places in Odisha I know of persons who have during their working life and also in retirement run to Khati like a mongoose to morphin or maybe even more strongly. There is an unparallel commitment to Khati time. No other social cause or event can wean serious khati participants away. About 15% of the time there is silence in Khati till one of the members is picked up for "riling". This 'riling' is fun and the binding factor. No value judgements, no holds barred, the riling or the teasing takes turns. About 80% time is spent on animated, excited opinions on politics, mostly current politics. If the khati has younger population then the discussions could get into the 'romance' space with even prescriptions thrown in generous doses for many 'romance related complexities'. Many get handholding support in Khatis. Communes are supposed to build communities. Khatis build clusters of cohesive groups, not necessarily always homogeneous, ready to stand by the group members. Funds support, networking for business development, marriage liaisons, health care issues get sorted out in a khati and through a khati. Cuttack khatis are traditionally so strong that they are known to run almost parallel to households. So strong is the call of khati that members forget chores to come and join Khatis during evenings. Families complain of neglect owing to Khati exhilaration. Such is the magnetism of Khati. Khati is liberating. It allows one to dream and share the dream. There is no official space provided to hold khati sessions but the parliament of khati sitting under a tree or a makeshift arrangement which eventually never shifts anywhere is the charm of a khati. It is not a club. It is an informal assembly with highest attachment and loyalty of members. There is nothing official about a khati. But the free, non caveat, human touch is the glue.

But corona would minimise our world, make us indoors and even more self-centred. Introspection, rest, rejuvenating are all officially correct words, but the reality is more TV watching, more time bent on tablets, more wasteful time on absurd social media, more binge eating, more consumption of ready-to-eat packaged food, spike in food and obesity related morbidities and demise of social life.

It seems we are completing a cycle – from solo wanderers in the forest to associations to solo existence amidst machines. From one jungle to the other but alone.

But you are asking me not to go to Khatti, not to call my Khatti friends and if we meet at all, then sanitise the Khatti. This is a tall order and a reductionist one.

I can't shrink. Let me go to Khatti and be with myself. Corona, please save my Khatti. It is Odisha's faith. We are always one in our Khatti.

■

Save Koraput : the Wonderland
(Koraput is the blessed land and the future of Asia)

Undivided Koraput district is the Wonderland. From Lord Jagannath to fighter planes to Asia's mineral treasury, it is complete & the people are content. Content because the tribals and their Lord live here. It is the sabar kshetra (the mystic land of the Lord). This is the land where divinity and materialism co-exist in a unique balance.

Over the last seven decades we have systematically neglected Koraput to serve our commercial interests. The outsiders who have plundered Koraput in the name of development have scant respect for the land and its people. The leading social organisations working in the district have more workers from other districts who have no belongingness to the place. They are working in Rayagada, Nawarangpur, Jeypore, and other areas since the last many decades and yet things have not improved in the districts. Per capita income of Koraput should be one of the highest in India, but sadly always figures in the list of 'aspirational districts" of Niti Ayog. The reserve of 310 million tons in Panchpatmali mines is world's largest single-site bauxite deposit and yet Koraput suffers the indignity of infant death, large scale migration and rapid forest destruction. In Koraput 79% live below poverty line.

Most of the government officers after retirement love to settle down in Koraput, but while in job have, they done enough for the Wonderland?

Blood Ore:

The tribes of Koraput are mute spectators to the mining blitzkrieg unleashed upon them. Let not the mining giant corporates make billions on the misery of Koraput adivasis.

Let's not stoke another Blood Ore !

Let's share the development and affluence. Now there is an overdrive in the country and Odisha for the auction of mines. But do we have a community development agreement ready to be signed with the mine owners, post auction? Importantly, do we think that a community development commitment is necessary? If yes, then who would decide or facilitate a plan which can be made mandatory for the prospective mine owners. As a part of the Action Plan (the master plan by the state), which am sure would have already been submitted to the Centre, the community development perspective would have been stitched together. I hope so.

There is a Sustainable Development Framework (SDF) to be ideally adopted by the mining companies. If it has not been made compulsory yet for the miners, it should be made so. The people of Koraput should ask for SDF of the mines.

It is impending and quite obvious that a huge land grab is threatening India's tribal people and that includes Koraput. This apparently looks like a bonanza for forest related industries and investments. The forest-dwelling adivasis, indigenous tribes, found in all the mining zones are the directly affected stakeholders under the SC order for the eviction of close to 2 million adivasis from protected forest lands across India. The claims of nearly 226,000 adivasi and other forest-dwelling households have been rejected on various grounds, including absence of proof that the land was in their possession for at least three generations.

But due to shocking laxity on our part, the tribals are deprived from getting the testimonials for their 'ownership' evidence. Citizen services facilitated by the district or state authorities could have prevented the adivasis staring at homelessness, any moment (over 15000 in Koraput). They are condemned to be refugees in their own land. Or are forced to out migrate as labour, humiliated, under paid and grossly deprived. The 'originals of the land" are relegated to an identity-less existence. Don't they belong to this country? Are they not our fellow citizens?

Is there any plan by the government or the miners to implement a systematic rehabilitation and resettlement program for the local communities? I am sure there would be an estimate of the displacement but is there a blueprint for tackling the displacement? Will the district authorities have the details?

Is it not our responsibility to rehabilitate them and handhold them to lead normal lives? OMC, Odisha Mining Corporation have had demonstrated commendable efforts in community outreach and sustainable mining - through installation of solar plants, use of solar street lights in the mines, rain water harvesting and ground water recharging at the mines, Installation of STP at their mines to re-cycle the waste water, Solar plants in mines to reduce the carbon foot prints and the like. But it is one thing to buck up initiatives in safe and sustainable mining practices and another to take care of the lives around mining areas in Koraput.

A Sustainable Development Framework would cover

lot many aspects and this includes comprehensive planning for the communities. Who is doing this or who is at least, planning to do this? The communities are not capable of even expressing their needs. The civil society organisations are outdated and dispassionately removed.

I have trust in the industry (the miners) to commission professional help in assessing the needs of the communities with the help of the district authorities. If at all, the District Collectorate is the governance, which is closest to the communities. If their capacities are worked upon then they could be the best point for monitoring of the i) Managing impacts at the mine level ii) Progressive mine closure & Landscape Restoration iii) addressing social impact and community engagement iv) reporting on sustainability, conducting social audits, energy audits etc.

The social subversion of the tribals, I have reasons to believe that these are not innocuous anymore, should not be allowed to dent deeper by the mining activities. SDF is not the panacea, nor is a part of the regulatory (it should have been) but it has the compass to cover comprehensively, all inclusive. The social aspects of development projects are usually the most challenging and can pose a significant risk to the successful implementation of projects. Because we are dealing with people with complex emotions, hopes, concerns, expectations and insecurities. Assessing a project's impact on the biophysical environment does not require any complicated processes. Mineral resources are finite and non-renewable, at least in biological timescales. Environmental, social problems along with mining related risks are increasingly breeding conflicts between miners and local communities. Understandably so.

Mining royalty is the biggest non-tax contributor to the Odisha's revenue stream pegged at Rs 6130.97 crore from production of 270.84 million tonnes (mt) and supply of 287.80 mt minerals in 2017-18. With the opening of the mines, the mining revenue is estimated to cross Rs 12,000 crore, 2021 onwards. The paradox is that education and agriculture term loans have the highest NPAs in the state. With the revenue from mining, the state should look at building parallel resources as standby. In about 5 decades from now all our reserves would be depleted and we would be an empty drum, ravaged and dumped. All the mineral-rich districts of the state featured in the list of most backward districts of the country. In Koraput, Asia's bauxite capital, 79 per cent live below poverty line. The income from mineral extraction has not benefitted the regions from where the minerals are removed. Rather poverty has increased in many of these districts like Koraput and has majorly affected the social fabric owing to quick gains due to the 'middlemen' syndrome.

If business looks for quid pro quo, so does the public.

Can we, the civil society of Koraput, be privy to the exploration plans of the bidding mining companies? Can we know about their blueprint for the mine's communities? Can all this be transparent and upfront? Can this be in public domain (on the department's web portal?)?

Rapidly changing global order, energy transitions, climate emergency and supersonic technological advancement should enable exemplary development of tribals of Koraput. ICTs (information & communication technologies) can be deployed for the development of the mines' communities. Because the mining in Odisha and specifically in Koraput would have global ramifications. The resources which would be sucked out are non-renewable. Can we squander away this opportunity and not build our lives, in the best possible manner?

If we don't take care of our tribals, the repository of our riches and spirituality, no amount of economic growth or GDP figures would be worthy, viable and pro human.

Where is the CSR?

The civil society of Koraput should come together and prepare a CSR White Paper which will help in providing the necessary framework for further integration of CSR in building a better framework of CSR in the District, helping to localise the SDGs (Sustainable Development Goals as set universally by the UN), with emphasis on social impact. The social license to operate is no more the sole driver. It's the human, environmental, societal and financial impact. The corporates don't have to do CSR to appease local people for social license to do business in Koraput. They have to genuinely contribute to Koraput's development.

In the last four years more than 1700 Cr has been deployed under CSR by about 280 plus companies. But the geographic spread of the CSR support to the communities across Odisha is not equitable. The state should take policy initiative to drive CSR as per the developmental needs of the districts/communities and that the corporates should be more proactive in "going beyond the walls". In terms of geographical coverage 6 districts (Malkangiri, Kandhamal, Nuapada, Boudh, Gajapati and Deogarh) with relatively lower human development index have been left out only because the companies do not operate in these areas. Whereas, Angul for example, a relatively developed district in the state, has alone received over 30% of the entire spending as it houses a good number of large industries. This regional disparity is because of the 'project area mindset' of the companies, and it does not serve the interest of Odisha.

The state through various mechanisms like the DMF,

CAMPA is expected to supplement local body finances by providing them with appropriate fiscal leverage. These funds are meant to be used by the state to implement agro-forestry in non-forest land to compensate for felled forest or for the benefit of the mining affected people of the state. All the forest dwellers and mining affected people belong to the tribals and marginalised sections and hence prudent deployment of the resources would help in dramatic reduction of poverty in Koraput. But at present more than Rs 3,500 Cr (more than 80% of the fund) DMF collection lie unspent or caught in red tapism. the DMF collections in various districts in 2015-16 was Rs 395.38 crore, in 2016-17, Rs 2109.89 crore and in 2017-18, Rs 1,670.31 crore. But the expenditure was a meagre 389.27 crore over the period. The DMF lying unused in Koraput district exceeds Rs 400Cr.

If industry-wise contribution is considered then Steel, Iron & Ferro alloys sector tops the list with over 40% spending, followed by Mining (20%) and Aluminium (20%) sectors. Maximum numbers of industries are in these sectors and in Koraput.

It is all about humans:

A recent study to evaluate neonatal and under-five mortality at district level and state level in India, indicates that in Rayagada the mortality rate is 141.7, probably the highest in the country. My fear is not solely based on the findings of the report, which could be further analysed and debated upon. But I am concerned about the ground level situation in spite of the Ama Sankalpa initiative, a targeted intervention program for reducing Infant Mortality Rate(IMR) and Maternal Mortality Rate(MMR). The district had taken path breaking drives like a) creating 14 additional delivery points for facilitating institutional delivery. b) identification of poor performing sub-centres c) household level identification of pregnant women and ensuring institutional delivery by line listing them at higher facilities like the CHC d) setting up Maa Gruha, where the pregnant mothers, specifically among the Particularly Vulnerable Tribal Group(PVTG) are housed for a week prior to the institutional delivery. Rayagada district is providing double fortified salt in the schools and anganwadi centres, containing iron and calcium to improve the nutritional status of adolescents, children and pregnant women. As one of the unique programs to tackle malnutrition, the Nutrition Rehabilitation Centre (NRC) under Sub-Divisional Hospital (SDH) at Gunupur has been upgraded from five bedded to ten bedded to accommodate severely acute malnourished children. The district has bike ambulance service available for ferrying pregnant women and critical patients from inaccessible areas like Kalyansinghpur block, Parsali under Niyamagiri Hill Range and Putasing where PVTGs like Dangaria Kandhas and Lanjia Sauras live, to hospitals. About 817 inaccessible pockets in the district have been identified where due to lack of roads, 102 and 108 ambulances cannot reach the villages.

Rayagada has major concentration of large size metals and extraction industries and hope and believe that this need and trend of growing commitment to sustainability and responsibility will mean that more companies would step up to address challenges outside the company. More companies will step up to help tackle the United Nations' Sustainable Development Goals. We'll see more corporations mapping the UN SDGs to their operations and values. It will be even more vital for companies to work together with states and NGOs to create value for societies, and in turn business opportunities that drive long-term, scalable value creation.

Gram Sabha in Koraput:

The mineral industry, specifically, depends on the indigenous rights and the development process, the principle of free, prior and informed consent (FPIC) derived from indigenous peoples' right to self-determination and their right to property through ownership or traditional use. How do the PVTGs in Koraput know what is good for them and not good before they take a decision? They should be informed and not mis-informed either by the industry or by the NGOs. At stake here is a reserve of 310 million tons, Panchpatmali mines, which is considered to be the world's largest single-site bauxite deposit. How many discussions have been organised with the local communities on this? How many of us know about the global ramifications of this process?

It seems that for the expansion project of NALCO, gram sabhas are being organised by the district administration in Maliput, Pottangi, Nuagaon and Kotia villages. The villagers, while putting forth their demands, favourably and unfavourably, voiced parameters to support the company to carry out mining and developmental activities. But do the villagers know what to ask for and what is their need? Is there any NGO or organisation there, to assist them assess their needs?

For the existing Panchpatmali bauxite mines, the Nalco has been awarded the highest 5-Star Rating of Government of India for its sustainable mining practices and environment protection measures. Do the affected or involved villagers know what this rating means? What is their inclusion in the development process? Have they been at least taken on a trip to show around how and what the company has done to adopt reclamation and rehabilitation processes for ecological restoration of the mined-out area? Is the area being systematically backfilled with lateritic overburden to form benches, terraces and leave-depressed area at strategic places to form reservoirs/ rainwater harvesting structures to support vegetation and wildlife. None of the villagers are aware of the process or the ensuing benefits of the processes.

Before the Gram Sabha sits, the people of the villages should know whether mine void has been reclaimed and afforested with trees of native species, having capacity to endure water stress and climatic extremes. Nalco's or any company's genuine efforts for environment protection also need to be disseminated amongst the direct affected people and not confined to the preserves of intellectual presentations in state capital and country capital.

This because Gram Sabha is where the action lies. It is the council holding the key to the development of the country. If Odisha is the gold mine and the global repository, Koraput is the vault, then Gram Sabha is the door to the treasure. More so, when we are discussing rental economy.

Nalco, with all its seemingly precautionary measures and pre-emptive steps to conserve nature and recharge water had to face opposition at the second Gram Sabha held at the panchayat office of Pottangi for the proposed bauxite mining. The locals feel that the local economy and household wellbeing of over 5,000 people of four panchayats depends on Serubandha hill and on minor forest produces. The local people use the stream water of the hills for agricultural activities. They are of the opinion that when mining starts, the streams will go dry and their economy will collapse. Who is there to spend time with

Serubandha Surakhya Samiti (which is spearheading the anti-mining movement) and share legitimate data, information and case studies to sensitise them? Their reaction should be genuine, and fact based, not political. The civil society has been under-performed in deep dive, long standing community intensive work. Can you name NGOs which work sustained with the community, notwithstanding external funds support? Taking CSR contracts for limited projects is the business of development, not development. Development needs dedication and not mediation.

Gram Sabha is probably our last, coveted democratic tool, working bottoms up. It would play a decisive role in charting a course for the future development of India. Gram Sabha would allow;

- Koraput and Odisha getting on to the fast lane of development
- Koraput & Odisha discarding its poverty tag and take on the high growth, 'smart' development brand
- The transition of natives from a forest-based dwelling to more mainstreaming, while maintaining equity and ecology
- The trade-off between reckless expansion (in the name of development) and real development in lives

Our last bastion of aboriginal simplicity and naivety should not be corrupted with manipulative systems which would rob them off their soil. This whole fight for international wealth making is for their soil. Gram Sabha would script our future growth story.

Koraput can majorly contribute to make Odisha a $1 trillion economy by 2030. After Maharashtra and Tamil Nadu Odisha could be the third State, by then, to be a $1 trillion economy.

Our intention is to provide enabling environment to business and not create stumbling blocks. But in the same vein, not to be cuckold.

Let's do true business.

Social work's diminishing returns

Social work in India has reduced itself to almost inaction. The government, the society needs social scientists and not parasites of fictitious poverty. This is a wake-up call and a commentary on a sector supposed to support mainstream economy and stand by the country in its hours of crises. Let us get the comatose third sector back to work because the returns presently are mere shadows of gram swaraj.

I would like to draw a parallel between the 'window of discourse' and the 'window of social work' in India. The Overton window, which is the first name of windows of discourse is the band of ideas around which acceptable public narratives and discourses are construed. The window implies that policymakers desist from venturing into areas uncharted for fear of rejection by the public, their masters. Similarly, social work in India operates within the frame of a window, hitherto unable to mainstream obscure ideas or changing goal posts or even going anywhere near 'innovations'. The complacency of 'going with the flow' is comfortable. With over 3.5 million NGOs in India, one for every 500 people, legitimately a sector has an enviable reach of at least 3X that of the government (imagine doctor to patient ratio 1:1456 or agri-extension officer to farmer ratio of 1:1162). Each NGO further fissions into many smaller nuclei groups of volunteers and community workers. It is the biggest platform of and for change. Investment in an NGO is by far the best guarantee to bring about mass scale behaviour change, practice reforms and running a self-reliant gram swaraj. The Gram Swaraj or sustainable rural autonomy can potentially weather the onslaught of climate emergencies, market volatility and tricky employment aspirations. An indispensable support to national life and character. With a blend of capital and human capital investments, the return from social work of the NGOs can be the highest ever and highest possible. But after seventy-three years, the NGOs are primarily implementing agencies, hardly ever willing to *jump* the windows of discourse. Yet, the sector boasts of relentless 'activists'. Where is the action or any disruption? What is this activism for? Maybe for self-eulogising awards, but that's not human development. It is self-development and good for them. The sector is yet to demonstrate the temerity to innovate with the world's largest population of below 30 and the world's burgeoning middle class? What are they waiting for?

    The civil society organisations (nee NGOs) spend over 90% of their time waiting for the next project announcement by a public service department to apply for a grant. Because they do not have their own programs or if there are, then the programs are designed to be a 'permanent outcome' of the public welfare program(s). The fit is perfect. Their scale of impact is directly proportional to their capacities in wooing the existing national and state programs, whether the beneficiaries want them, need them or not. The 'beneficiary' is blurred in this case because over 75% of the budget (from the grant) is spent on staff salaries. Who is the beneficiary in this case?

The rate of conversion of specific needs of a demography into a full-fledged, targeted intervention is well below 10% - one in 10 current needs of the community is targeted by the social development programs. Government schemes are well planned but poorly executed because a) NGOs lack basic capacities to implement b) there is no ownership of the schemes c) the Collectors get transferred frequently and the collectorate is ill equipped in terms of professional manpower and skills. The Collector *owns* a district and s/he rarely get support from NGOs in implementation and feedback. Community needs change rapidly, but the methodologies have never changed after the late eighties, and early nineties when India embarked upon a slew of health programs with the help of the multilateral and bilateral support. The same flip charts, FGDs, above-the-line and below-the-line approaches and materials are used till date, cornball, unimaginative, and uninspiring. Nothing much has changed since the JNU alumni took to social work. New institutions, ideas get buried below a quick job in CSR department. The young MSWs/MBAs/IITans brim with possibilities but are yet to know the market – the recipients of their models. They learn go-to-market theories in the classrooms and leave them behind.

What happens after ASER is published? Barring a few interventions in states like Rajasthan, Maharashtra and a few others, STEM for example, has not been taken up rigorously as a thrust area. For example, Children need assistance with their psycho-social barriers in learning mathematics and their trepidations. Only giving ICT based, video lessons is tokenism and is not the solution. The future minds of this world continue to wade their way through lacklustre, painful, obscure education. The human touch is absent. No wonder AI & ML are already in the room. Social work has now turned into contract work? Prominent NGOs of India are building houses, roads because that adds to their balance sheet and not to their core strength. Should we expect builders to be NGOs? So then rightfully, the government has decided to make GST compulsory for NGOs.

NGOs should be the laboratories with social scientists along with MSW/MBA qualified program managers. If all will manage, who will ideate? This will soon lead to a BPO wave in social work, without an iota of innovations, barring a few mediocre attempts to create mobile phone apps or data collection spreadsheets in the name of technology interventions. The MSW is expected to help the welfare schemes of the country (the government) to reach the unreached and utilised in tandem with the intentions. Leakages in welfare schemes have not helped us reduce poverty the way the government has committed to in the SDGs. The livelihoods programs in states like Odisha, Rajasthan, AP, Telangana are doing well with new, unfamiliar approaches. New age social work should bring fresh perspectives to the large sums of taxpayers money being invested in low income groups. An effective deployment of this money will mean reduced social strain between haves and have nots. Is this not the fundamental ideology of the self-claimed activists? But are they helping in the professional development of social workers? The students should realise the significance of social work, their chosen career path – that they can and should function like a professional conduit or a gateway to redistribute income from the young to the elderly, from taxpayers to subsidy recipients and from the rich to the poor. One rupee spent on social work at one end should deliver an impact of at least 2000X at the other end. They would be responsible for at least 13% of the GDP which is government spending in India with impact at such a mega scale. The economics of social work is by far the most powerful link between an underdeveloped and developed economy. This potential of the sector is squandered. A national social forum like CII or FICCI , with predominantly young social workers, is part of the answer. There is a tragic vacuum in civil society leadership in the country, in thought or action. Civil society is both the universe and the workshop and is much more than only the third sector if you may. Return from any investments here will easily be the highest, unmatched, and limitlessly sustainable. Yet we miss the simple markers. It is the most potent of all change vehicles but is presently antiquated and mostly off road.

Are we here to lament a lost paradise or disrupt and recentre to create an evergreen Eden? the choice is ours. It might be too early for my epitaph but contributions to GDP and GHI is still awaited. The country is looking for me and my fellow shenanigans in social work.

■

Micro planning in Odisha, post- COVID

I am not sure when is the end of COVID or if it has an end at all. The virus attack from high risk groups is now entering into the general population and its menace is getting bigger and bigger every day. Not only the spread, but its 'easiness' in contagion, is paralysing. One need not do anything complicated or severely risky to get the attack. A mere touch or proximity even without a touch is enough to kill. So uncannily it resembles the remote killing button often seen in sci-fi movies. Population and communities are getting wiped off as we gather momentum to resist. This requires individual restrain in movement. But in many 'supposedly' disciplined countries, the communities have so far been the most unruly. They have been responsible for the morbidities to spread, and killings, to a large extent.

In Odisha, the ground-breaking idea of Panchayats handling the registration and monitoring of the migrants actually puts the management of the community in the hands of the community. Under a pandemic, I would rate this move as one of the most audacious and progressive.

While the Panchayat is going to be the repository of the data of the last mile, it makes sense for them to plan and implement youth development programs. After the migrants' home coming, the next immediate challenge would be the livelihoods. Panchayats do not have the capacity to prepare livelihoods blueprints and would need help. The civil society organisations of Odisha, most of which are only welfare program managers and that too short term. Handling more than half a million migrants needs large number of localised micro plans.

Odisha should be the first state to demonstrate that the Gram Swaraj model of Gandhiji works because the state has a strong Panchayati raj system which is working, albeit the challenges of proxy leadership by husbands of women panchayat leaders and sporadic financial leakages. But in comparison to many other states in India, rural Odisha is well set for development programs. The programs need to be initiated from Bhubaneswar to make Panchayats own, via the District Collectorates. The 6798 Gram Panchayats of Odisha and the identified 7276 Temporary Medical Camps in all these GPs should continue to be the outreach centres and eventually made permanent centres. COVID's aftermath will be long term and would need a lot of behaviour change and risk mitigation to be adopted by the people. These centres could operate as multilevel service centres because going forward the youths would need constant engagement. Their joblessness will create destabilising social and economic problems.

The State Planning Board should be put into action to make micro plans for the Panchayats. The Board can make the plan with the help of the local organisations/ agencies. Think tanks like FIDR can assist the government in making professional plans which would be acceptable by Banks, Government agencies for subsequent funding and business support to the youths. NABARD would need viable proposals to support agriculture activities. This year's Rabi harvest lies waste and could not reach the market and the Kharif preparation looks uncertain. Outward migration would reduce if initiatives are immediately taken to make agriculture and allied sectors more viable and sustainable for the farmers. The state has a cultivated area of 61.80 lakh hectares with more than 91% of these belonging to small and marginal category and the average size of land holding is 1.04 hectare. So, a careful plan, with adequate financing, involving technology and smart marketing is required to increase productivity and farmer income. Per capita availability of land, water and other natural resources is diminishing along with the various biotic (insect and diseases) and abiotic stresses (natural disasters - flood, drought, cyclone etc.), increasing poverty and migration. This is the best time to gear up, make micro plans, influence banks, and proliferate rural Agri-entrepreneurship. It is not farming but also selling and making profits. Jajpur district which is expecting more than 50000 migrants to come back to the district has about 1,30,000 hectors in paddy land during the forthcoming Kharif season and is also known for high quality groundnut and horticulture. The rehabilitation of the migrants is of immediate concern and agriculture is the sector which they can get absorbed in before the other industries in Jajpur area reopen. Resumption of manufacturing units would take some time, and, in the meantime, agriculture could prove gainful employment. Similarly, in Ganjam.

In other places of Odisha with access to IT/ITeS and reasonable internet connectivity, the youth should be oriented to online learnings in AI and machine learning.

After COVID, Cybercrime and impingement would be a growing area of work, much bigger than what it is today. The days of human intermediaries is numbered, even if it exists in some sectors now. COVID 19 made the grounds more fertile for AI and ML to grow faster and voracious. As the COVID-19 coronavirus outbreak continues to proliferate and gets entrenched, researchers are looking to use artificial intelligence as a way of addressing the challenges of the virus. Our original intelligence falls short and the projects are using AI to address the coronavirus outbreak. Many research projects are using AI to identify drugs that were developed to fight other diseases, but which could possibly be now repurposed to fight COVID. AI helps in studying the molecular setup of existing drugs and identifies the ones which could disrupt COVID-19's attack. So, after COVID, we cannot but completely rely on AI to save us from pandemics and attacks. In the near future a lot of requirements would come from this sector along with the specialised pharma and our boys and girls should be prepared for that.

Besides agriculture, IT and pharma are the industries which are promising in the post-COVID days. This might look daunting but can be done by setting up rural BPMs - The Impact Sourcing model not only reduces adult digital illiteracy rates drastically but also creates thriving rural communities. Half a million migrant workers are heading Odisha way soon and the state has so far created 2.27 lakh beds in 7276 isolation facilities. All returnees will be mandatorily sent for 14 days of quarantine to these facilities. Every quarantined person will be stamped with date in indelible ink. The government is ready to bear the cost towards food, health, and accommodation of the people. Upon completion of 14-days of quarantine, each person will be given incentive of Rs. 2000. The same level of preparation is necessary for the engagement of the people who would now stay in Odisha, mostly permanently. They would have nowhere to go for at least about a couple of years.

And from now on Odisha needs to step up agriculture, engage youth and retain power with the Panchayat to minimise COVID's menace on its economy. Micro planning is the first step.

■

We have failed Mr. Akshaya Mohanty

Our adulation is only superficial it seems. Akshaya Mohanty is omnipresent in our lives – from WhatsApp, FB to events & all kinds of music banters, non-music khatis, everywhere across three generations. He is supposed to be the king of Odia modern music, the fountainhead of modernity and out-of-the-closet romance in Odia music. Some of us believe that he was much more than a only a musician or a music maker. He made every Odia household spread their wings, break the staid middle-class coyness, and he himself was larger than life. He was the trendsetter, a maverick personality, then quite rare in a bottled-up society. Girls had crush on him. It is rumoured that elders also were attracted. The attraction was the unique combination of trendy music, high quality but uncomplicated expressions and free spirited persona. His ORB 222 ambassador car with him at the wheels was a trailblazer in Buxi bazaar, which was his major joint. His candour took our society by storm. His experiments with his writings and music were audacious. He was an iconoclast in many ways. He stormed the cringy music bastion, dominated by Calcutta studios, with a freshness, unknown, unheard. He took music not to the classrooms of Sangeet Vidyalayas and gurus but to where it belongs – the heart.

He released Odia music and romance, in verse, out of the asphyxiation of prudish lyrics and subverted expressions. But why are we so nostalgic about Mr Mohanty? Do we truly respect him? He has given Odia culture a new direction, a new whiff of air.

Yet, we don't want him to win any recognition, forget Padma Award.

Yet, we forget to give him any return gift but sing paeans in WhatsApp Messages & social media which are essentially lifeless and repetitions. The messages are drowned and swamped every second, every day and every year.

We listen to his oft repeated numbers, never ever bother to read about him or touch upon new perspectives of his life or thinking. There is no research instituted for his body of work, which is not only versatile but far reaching – from folk, devotional to modern, romantic and brilliant prose. His thoughts reflected the restlessness of the youth of the 70s and 80s. But where is the documentation? Where is a Research chair in the University?

His erstwhile hangers on organise events which we are better off without, due to their sub-standard quality and presentations.

Everything about celebrations in his name, has now become trite, absolutely a rigmarole, heartless and ritualistic.

Everyone in WhatsApp seem to know him – the generic Bhai, but most neglected. He is made to be like the proverbial joker of a circus who's there to entertain you for the evening, giving his sweat and blood and not getting even a pat in return. The perennial "kalankita nayak".

His writings are urbane, magnificently uncomplicated, extremely Odia in spirit but stylish in presentation. If translated, his writings can easily become national.

We, the diaspora remember him – twice or thrice in a year. The same numbers, the same speeches about him, the same attempts to establish the speaker's "personal connect" with Khoka bhai and the same forgetting dear Khoka bhai after the show. A little high, we only remember "punyara nadi teere" and the next moment he is out of our radar.

I am responsible for utterly neglecting him, using him, ditching him and dropping his name in every conversation.

I am asking myself; do we deserve the cult – Mr Akshaya Mohanty?

Stop calling him Khoka Bhai if you stop honouring him. Someday we will realise what it means to be a lover. Till then I continue to be a self-centred, boorish and a fake connoisseur. I have done nothing for Mr Akshaya Mohanty, the culture icon of modern Odisha.

If this is not absolute banality, what is?

Learn to call him Mr Akshaya Mohanty, not Khoka Bhai. Brotherhood's sanctity is something we have not yet internalised and respected.

■

Mission "Clean Puri"

The blackmail has been blunted. This is no mindless endorsement of the demolition drive around Jagannath temple in Puri. The pulling down of dilapidated structures overcrowding the precincts of the Lord of the Cosmos is a rare bold step, taken after centuries of 'slumming'. The mathas around the Puri temple need to be razed because the Jagannath temple needs more fortification and tidying which is overdue. Some 5-6 centuries ago these mathas (also the other mathas in general) were intended to impart Sanskrit lessons to young scholars, visiting scholars, offer boarding facilities for pilgrims and offer specialised services to the rituals of Jagannath temple. Many of these mathas had good libraries at some point in time. I have visited many but now the scholastic relevance of the mathas is completely absent and desiccated.

In early days the mathas in Puri were built and supported by 'Lines of Following" and so Ramanuja Acharya, a seer of Shaivanism set up Emar mutt or Ramananda founded the Bada Akhada matha with the purpose of preparing servitors with physical training to guard the temple and its sanctity. The seers or religious leaders who established mathas did so with the help of the rulers and rich patrons. The land and the donations that these mathas received belong to the people. The mathas originally meant to be learning and spiritual centres have become centres of conflicts – litigations on Mahanta succession, ugly tussles over property ownership (they own huge tracts of land) and uncountable hording of gold, precious stones and riches. Mathas are of the seers, by the seers and for the learners. Where is the play of slabs of gold in this? Is this why the mathas should squat over swathes of land both near the temple and in farmlands in villages? The Puri Gazetter describes thus, the "Mathas are monastic houses originally founded with the object of giving religious instructions to chelas or disciples and generally of encouraging a religious life." Sreemandir is perhaps the only temple on planet earth which propounds the tenet that 'all humans are one'. The oneness is seen in practice, not only in rhetoric. The patrons including feudal lords, kings, traders from all over had put up 752 mathas to accommodate pilgrims from all over the world and provide food & comfort without commercial purposes. This is also believed to be the inspiration behind the 'Langar' service of the Gurudwara culture. Guru Nanak had established Bauli matha in Puri which is in ruins now, almost.

To put it straight, mathas are irrelevant today and could not meet the high purposes they were meant for. How many of you or the ones who are shouting for the preservation of the mathas have ever been inside a matha in Puri? They are inhabitable. They provide inhuman quarters (dormitories) to pilgrims (who choose to stay there now) and even to the poor and hapless widows during Kartika brata.

The mathas were revered once upon a time as the

gateway or the stop overs to the ultimate unison with Lord Jagannath. But they have lost all significance because they could not retain their coveted position of postulating adwait doctrine. How many below 35 would even know what a matha is? How would they know when we do not know anything about mathas nor the mathas have ever chosen to be in the mainstream? When it comes to street fights, we remember 'preserving culture and legacy of Puri'.

How many civil society organisations have ever taken up the cause of mathas (if there was any cause) and have helped restore them?

When were you in a matha, last?

Shreekshetra is one of the seven most holy places for Hindus in the globe and is one in the four Dhams (Char Dham) considered to be the highest zones for Hindu faith. Cleaning of the Dham will set an example for the rest of the world to preserve such old temples of faith, which steer humanity.

The Garuda Purana says,

Ayodhyâ Mathurâ Mâyâ Kâsi Kâñchî Avantikâ I
Purî Dvârâvatî chaiva saptaitâ moksadâyikâh II

(the seven holy places of Hindu faith)

The religious mathas are always seen as rigid institutions that preserve old traditions and not as ones that are in sync with the changing times or norms. They have never been able to transform into institutions that can connect with society while changing with times. They could not evolve because of their limited capabilities and intellectual proclivities. A matha today is nothing more than a building because they are bereft of the divine spirit. If it is a decrepit building, then why should it stand between me and my Lord?

I support the state's incredible and unparallel

decisiveness in cleaning the muck around our Lord's abode. In many old cities with similar situations around the world, I have noticed that the administrations have not been bold enough to bulldoze encroaching structures. What Odisha has done today in Puri, the rest of the country would follow. In complete solidarity with the plucky and progressive move of the State.

The abode of the Lord of the Cosmos has to be the brightest, strongest and the nattiest. Because that is the least, we mortals (and Odias) can offer as our reverence and prayer. Keep our highest pedestal clean, safe and long lasting.

On one hand I can't pillory the sanitation and infrastructure of Puri and on the other turn activist overnight for the mathas.

We cannot neglect our Lord for decadent mathas. No way.

Hats off Odisha !

The Devdas effect

Devdas Chhotray has survived tectonic shifts in Odia living and thinking and yet has remained unfazed. Because his language is one of positivity and celebrations, primarily and quite intrinsically. We need to realise the effect of his work and not his work only. His lexicon in Odia from 'nai tutha' (ନଈତୁଠ) or 'golapi chithi' (ଗୋଲାପିଚିଠି) which might sound retro romance now, was liberating romance, much ahead of his times. Urbane and a sophisticate, Devdas finds solace in that romance in the hinterlands of Odisha, which he juxtaposes in urban Odisha. He has come out of Cuttack, travelled far and wide, but Cuttack has not exited him. It cannot. Being the son of Gopal Chhotray, student times in the colourful Ravenshaw college, early induction into the laboratory of Akshaya Mohanty, the attention he got as a young, donnish and yet a romantic writer is perhaps stuff dreams are made of, anywhere and more so in Odisha of the 60's. He never lost his balance with the early celebrityhood in his life and probably that is why his everlasting composure. Master storyteller, he captivates with his simplicity in prose, poetry, screenplay, lyrics. We know that he rescued Odia literature from the clutches of pedantic, obfuscate and complicated expressionism.

He simplifies because he writes from his heart. A more head ruled bouquet could have landed a few more awards on his well-appointed study. That might have perched him at the "supposedly high table" of Odia literature. Much before the coronation, he was already the darling in every corner of the state and the diaspora. Quite akin to the journey of his senior guide, Akshaya Mohanty – they both lived in every Odia and less at Rabindra Mandap. Some geniuses are not meant to be award savvy.

Devdas Chhotray has made Odia literature fluid and flowing. He is the changemaker and a quiet, non rabid that too. Hence his style has never gone out of fashion. Youngsters love him. Mamta, a young IT professional in USA and my friend sends video messages with his (lyrics) songs because she says that she can 'connect' with him. Otherwise many like her would never attempt to identify with Odia literature. Here is a litterateur whose work does not stagnate or intimidate. Odisha Sahitya Academy award for a maverick, bold, culture changemaker would certainly open doors for more experimentation. Odia intellectualism, across fields, warrants freshness in approach and mindset. It is now an existential issue.

So original is his craft that he hardly uses his professional title (IAS) as a support to seek legitimacy as a thinker. This is a rarity. He is known as what he is - Devdas Chhotray, and that is enough. His fans across geographies notice this and get even more awed.

The creator of 'Nila Saraswati', 'Mallika', 'Lal Machcha', 'Hati saja kara' and obviously 'Rama ku maribara panchati upaya' has stood firm in a literary firmament which strangely endorses priggish trends many times and to date. He is undaunted because he has no feud, is disarmingly original in thinking, is diverse in his taste and is tremendously futuristic. That is why he is 'tomorrow's litterateur'.

GenZ cannot escape the Devdas effect. He is the culture changemaker of our times – subtle, genteel, and unmistakably powerful.

■

Mines reservation & Odisha's bargain

As expected, the metal industry investors are now clamouring for guarantee from the state for regular supply of their raw materials. This makes business sense but the intention, unilateral. The tone of such a recent demand was somewhat 'jarring'. They claim that their presence in the state has contributed to the development of the people and hence the state should guarantee unhindered flow of raw materials. In short, they should be handed over the mines.

The deal must be a win-win.

The corporates have made investments following their own board decisions. They have come to Odisha because they see opportunities to increase their profitability and scale up their growth. When the reservation of the mines is discussed across the table in Bhubaneswar, the state should draw up a detailed account of the dividends the people of Odisha have received because of the investments.

Negotiations have to be in the interest of the state, as the natural resources on which is based the growth story of future Odisha are irreplaceable or un-replenishable. This is the biggest gamble for the State. The investments are queuing up because Odisha is rich below the soil. Without our minerals, we can't aim at a $1 trillion economy. I have written earlier about this.

Almost 25% of the country's iron and manganese ore resources will be up for sale for captive users and merchant miners. By doing so Odisha, the projected steel capital of India would be the principal provider to India's targeted 300mt steel capacity by 2030. Odisha's mines have a direct influence on the economy of India and world trade. India, the world's second-largest steel producer is now a net importer. If we deal smartly and business-like, Odisha would never be the same again. I foresee our State to be a global destination.

If the corporates claim that with their investments, they have been able to increase local employment then that should be ratified by the local labour office and the Collector. The District Collector should be a part of the discussions with the corporates regarding the reservation of mines. The local civil society is an important stakeholder. It is the primary stakeholder. But are they ever party to such life-altering decisions or discussions? The gram sabhas should be discussing about the reservation of mines. Mines belong to the 'custodian communities'. How can a few on the high stools in Bhubaneswar or Delhi decide on the largesse to the corporates?

If the corporates are given the mines, can we ensure, with a bond, that they would be responsible for the development of the district or the state or the PHCs of the district or the colleges of the district or the NACs? Can we fix responsibilities with timelines and checkpoints? CSR programs, so far, have been glorious on paper, barring a few. If at all, only one-third of the state is benefitting inequitably from CSR. The activities are not planned as per any developmental needs assessment. They are random and are often implemented as knee jerk sops to propitiate irate local communities. This spoil and skews the ethos of the communities too and their aspirations.

Investment in the state and concomitant creation of employment should not be viewed as any form of 'generosity' by the corporates. Their investments in Odisha has given tremendous boost to their market capitalisation. Many have, overnight become Indian multinationals by dint of their Odisha operations. Odisha has given them their identity.

If their investments have yielded employment, then the numbers should speak. "Employment of thousands" is a pompous statement. The local household incomes must have had grown manifold, if they have employed 'thousands'. Do we have the data? Who have done the surveys? Can we have assessments by independent state based agencies?

We understand the need for supply assurances by the state for such mega projects. Pragmatically speaking, the investments would go awry if the supply is interrupted. So, their proposal for reservations of mines is prudent and expected. But not with any perspective of 'extortion' from the state. In a rental economy, the proposal should be equally rewarding to both the parties – the investor and the state. In a few decades from now, when the resources are exhausted, what do we do? Our communities are the primary stakeholders and they should invest in gilt edge securities. Where is our security?

Mining royalty is the biggest non-tax contributor to the state's revenue stream pegged at Rs 6130.97 crore from production of 270.84 million tonnes (mt) and supply of 287.80 mt minerals in 2017-18. With the opening of the mines, the mining revenue is estimated to cross Rs 12,000 crore, 2021 onwards. Education and agriculture term loans have the highest NPAs in the state. With the revenue from mining, the state should look at building parallel resources as standby. In about 5 decades from now all our reserves would be depleted and we would be an empty drum, ravaged and dumped. All the mineral-rich districts of the state featured in the list of most backward districts of the country. In Keonjhar, the epicentre of mining , 62 per cent of the population lives below poverty line. In Koraput, Asia's bauxite capital, 79 per cent live below poverty line. The income from mineral extraction has not benefitted the regions from where the minerals are removed. Rather poverty has increased in many of these districts and has majorly affected the social fabric owing to quick gains due to the 'middlemen' syndrome.

If business looks for quid pro quo, so does the public.

All of us, please let's not fritter away our natural wealth. If we are indifferent, lackadaisical and ignorant, we would be even much poorer and deprived than now.

Please negotiate evidence based, hard and data centric. Our intention is to provide enabling environment to business and not create stumbling blocks. But in the same vein, not to be cuckold.

Let's do real business.

True Independence & NEP 2020

NEP 2020 is the new tool which will change India forever and liberate young minds, who constitute most of India today. 1947, 1991 and 2020 are the three milestones in the timeline of this nation which have shaped the lives of India more directly and the life of the globe, directly.

NEP is a tool which needs to be implemented as planned. Otherwise, it would remain a smart tool. Tool needs to be used. It is expected to usher in unprecedented flexibility in our education programs, liberalise the career choices and completely change the face of our education eco system. I sincerely believe that with the introduction of the innovative approach, the new templates and wider options towards work and life, the rote system will be done away with. The brave introduction of experiential learning is going to be the differentiator.

Under NEP, NISHTHA (National Initiative for School Heads and Teachers Holistic Advancement), which is arguably the world's largest teachers' training programme of its kind, will motivate and equip teachers to encourage and foster critical thinking in students'. This is an unprecedented reform in teachers' capacities and pedagogy delivery. So far teachers are one of the worst neglected in our country. While there was regular thinking about the outcomes of the children's education, not enough attention was given to the teachers' upgradation in competencies and their exposure to newer teaching and guiding methods and tools.

NEP 2020 sets a new agenda for the country. Bharat will shift from an education policy whose focus was on primary school system through 'operation blackboard' to a skill-oriented education. This way the education would contribute 'tangibly' to the economy of the country. This change has been in accordance with the changing global demands. NEP 2020 now aims to make our education more globally apt, suitable and need based. The move towards a more liberal approach has the potential to positively impact the psyche of the coming generation and will strengthen the building blocks of the country. Unfortunately, on the provider's side, the teachers' presence, mostly till the secondary levels had almost been shadowy and they have been historically made to get involved in activities, other than teaching related. NEP looks at refurbishing their identities and bringing back the lost eminence of teachers. Teachers build the nation and NEP aims at according them, the due respect.

I am sure by 2035 we would have more students and also faculty from underrepresented sections, minority community education institutes, foraying contribution to innovations in the true sense. NEP augments Atmanirbhar Bharat by ensuring quality, quantity and diversity in skill building. We are going to introduce vocational courses for children and relieve the school students of the "bagful of rote days" in school. NISHTHA would help the entire eco system meet the growing and multifarious requirements of the young minds. The teachers will be sensitised and will develop their skills on various aspects related to Learning Outcomes, Competency Based Learning and Testing, Learner-focused Pedagogy, School Safety and Security, Personal-social qualities, and Inclusive Education.

In the immediate next two decades digital learning for students and ICT readiness of teachers will be as necessary as rudimentary alphabets. Unavoidable. Teachers, under NISHTHA should get awareness on ICT in teaching-learning including Artificial Intelligence, Health and well-being including yoga, Initiatives in School Education including library, eco club, youth club, kitchen garden, School Leadership qualities, Environmental Concerns, Pre-school, Pre-vocational Education and School Based Assessment in a joyful learning manner. So, while the teaching sector would get much more quality-centric and contemporary, their diversity will be both in specialisation and also in generalisation. Teaching as a profession would regain its lost glory and would prove much more lucrative (legitimately).

The combination of skilling with theory will open avenues to young minds right from school level to skill themselves through vocational courses. But I am also equally hopeful that this will develop a cadre of highly skilled teachers and the cascading effect will show in a short time because the policy is a conscious step to transform India into a knowledge hub. There is an ideal blend of the ethos of Indian philosophy, and sustainable development goals in the proposed curriculum at the undergraduate level. RTE with Inclusive education right from foundation till the professional stage will be Bharat's asset in the times to come.

NEP allows complete flexibility to the students by offering the exit-re-entry option in HEIs, credit transfer across universities to find the compatibility and according all streams equal weightage. Young minds do not have to suffer any more in rigid compartmentalisation. Similar to the ivy league and reputed global institutions, NEP opens up vistas for the Universities and encourages fundraise from corporates and governments on the basis of research work and innovations. The faculty would now be accessing much more avenues and opportunities to do wide range of research work, innovations and breakthrough patents.

The Policy brings much-awaited reforms and regulatory framework which will meet the needs of a 21st century 'New India' and create a bright, fertile and energetic environment. Teachers would get remarkable opportunities to build their capacities at world levels. Students would experience a complete change in learning environment, but so would also the teachers and faculty members. While talking about the students let's not forget our revered teachers. The time has come for them to go global. Our teachers should be guiding world education.

The first phase of teachers' trainings, under NISHTHA, will be conducted directly by 33120 Key Resource Persons (KRPs) and State Resource Persons (SRP). They would be identified by the State and UTs. The resource persons would be trained by 120 National Resource Persons chosen from National Council of Educational Research and Training (NCERT), National Institute of Educational Planning and Administration (NIEPA), KVS, NVS, CBSE and Non-Government Organisations.

This rigour is expected to build the capacities of around 42 lakh participants covering all teachers and Heads of Schools at the elementary level in all government schools, faculty members of State Councils of Educational Research and Training (SCERTs), District Institutes of Education and Training (DIETs) as well as BRC (Block Resource Coordinators) and CRC (Cluster Resource Coordinators) in all states and UTs. Let us help NEP create new India.

If this is not nation building, what is?

■

On JPD
(Jagannath Prasad Das)

He stands tall, unbending in his demeanour and stature in the journey since the late forties (1949) when his first poem was published in Kumkum. So much like a scuba diver, he dives deep, is self-contained and perennially observant. A typical litterateur of his times in Odisha or of Odisha origin fell into two brackets – civil servant and non-civil servant. He chose not to two-time his first love, literature and quit the elite Indian administrative career, for which he prepared in the then "Oxford of the east", Allahabad University. He taught at the University too and is known among peers, juniors, seniors as a brilliant student, topper in MA. All through from his Banapur early school days he has been a topper. Passion warrants compromise. The could-have-been Cabinet Secretary of India, chucked it all and pursued writing. I have never ever heard him brag this. Probably because greatness comes in simple steps, steps which we find daunting and unthinkable in an Odia household. An administrative service job, in Odisha is considered nothing short of a 'lightening from the skies' and the 'greatest benediction' in life. More so in the late fifties when he was 22. His first poem collection was published seven years before his joining IAS. Many turn writers after they secure their material comforts as an officer, but he wrote because that was his natural calling since Banpur and Cuttack school days, when he topped in his class and dared dream through his classroom windows. He is a dreamer and yet quite 'still'. I have found this combination, exuding through his piercing eyes, quite astonishing.

His Saraswati Samman recognised his first love, poetry - " let me say in poetry, all that I want to say, " and his seminal Prathama Purusha changed the quality of readership in Odia. Invincible, it is difficult to influence him – in ideologies, roller-coaster trends or with the insecurities of awards as the stamp of greatness. He has stood his ground, honourably and unobtrusively.

JPD is certainly a non-conformist but not an iconoclast or a complainant. This is unique. He thinks that Odisha is full of budding intellectuals and currently there are many templates and formats to express creativities and not necessarily only print writing, which was the inevitability of his times. He is as comfortable as ever, living now in Bhubaneswar after having spent decades in Lutyens Delhi amidst the culturati of India and evenings at India International Centre, his favourite haunt for many decades. With him doyens like Mulk Raj Anand, Gulzar, Ravi Baswani, Nissim Ezekiel and others have been in consistent conversation but have never awed him. That reflects his respect for individual and collective spaces. He belongs to the old guard and yet he does not. Rarely does he dwell in the past. This in itself is a rarity and happens to people, immersed in work, incessantly. Currently he is engaged in penning a new novella, after a long time. The pollution of Delhi has played havoc with his health and had to take short sabbaticals from writing.

JPD flirts with formats - poetry, plays, short stories, novel, essays, children's poems. A renaissance man, JPD started at a time when competition among Odia writers was acute. Though civil but the range was limited and hence the race to be visible was often quite mean and political. But JPD spent almost all his time in researching and digging facts and not racing. One can sense his almost meditative engagement in Desha Kala Patra, a novel but historical, based on the changing social mores and times in late 19th century. Vikram Seth's Suitable Boy was published a year later and by then I had finished this six-hundred-page novel, a treat in romancing vintage Odisha and its different shades of life. It is a literary classic and deservingly has been translated into various Indian languages.

Odia literature suffers from a severe dearth in translations – both Odia to other languages and vice versa. Barring Nandini Satpathy, Ananta Patnaik and a few others Odia writers rarely translated or got translated. The culture of a state does not get ventilation without translation. JPD's contribution to Odisha culture and its dissemination can be gauzed form his body of translation works - translated Odia Women Poets' Work into English, Catherine Clement's poems into English, Gulzar's poems from Urdu into English, Werner Aspenstrom's poems into Odia, Lakshmipurana into English and more. When I quizzed him specifically about his choice of Lakshmipurana as he is a self-confessed atheist, his repartee was that "it is about the evil of untouchability and gender atrocity" in one story. He does not wear atheism on his sleeves, nor does he make it his brand. He is as 'matter of fact' as always and as in everything else in his life. While translating many international literatures into Odia he has worked with names like Arlene Zide, the French writer Catherine Clement, the Swedish poet Werner Aspenstrom and K.Satchidanandan.

So, he might have churned less titles in all these decades (over five decades) but each one of his is considered a master craft because of the detailed collocations with the times and the nuances. His plays Suryasta Purbaru, Saba Sesha Loka , Sunderdas have been staged at the national levels, included in the repertoire of NSD, JNU and translated to other languages including English. JPD has acted on stage, albeit in cameo roles but has been a keen practitioner of arts, in various forms. Not sure whether he ever had any interest in fine arts, but his association with cinemas has been remarkable. His examination of Patta Chitra is considered a ground-breaking reference compendium on the most famous style of painting in Odisha. Besides holding positions - national Film award jury member or board member children's film society of India, his love for films and discussions about them is intense and valued.

Jagannath Prasad Das has been an eminence grise of Odia literature. Much beyond the awards (Central Sahitya Academy award which he refused, Nandikar Award for plays, the Sarala Award for short stories and the Saraswati Samman, he is a mentor to many young writers and thinkers. Because he does not carry any baggage of basking in past glories, he is mentoring many young minds of Odisha. Very contemporary, JPD school has a distinct identity. It is walking the fine line between the romance of imagination and factual juxtaposition. Reality and romance travelling together is a unique trip.

Unfailingly I try to meet him at Bhubaneswar, as often as possible, and almost always take an enthusiast along with me. The more we hear him, the more we get enlightened.

Time has come when we need to foster a tank of thinkers in Odisha – young and new age. JPD is the culture rebbe (not confined to literature only). Odia society is in immediate need of creative oxygen. Leafing through Jagannath Prasad Das legacy is like visiting a bright room with many windows to different worlds – letters, thoughts, drama, cinema, history, culture and as many as we can mine. Poetry books, short stories, Odia plays, Odia novels, childrens' literature, anthologies, research papers, essays, English translations, Odia translations, the inventory is both wide and deep. Many more are in the offing.

His parents had named him appropriately – Jagannath Prasad, gift of the Lord. I am sure he would dismiss this simile, as self-effacingly as always.

■

Kotia Panchayat is our family

The urgency in enfolding Kotia Panchayat.

We are blessed because we have Koraput which is the wonderland of India and is the resource capital – treasure below soil and Lord Jagannath above. Koraput and its people reflect Odisha in many ways – their naivety, comity, and divine simplicity. The world is coming to Koraput - for gold, platinum, manganese, bauxite, graphite and limestone. We need to have our plans for responsible use of the resources and concomitant development of the people. Any industrialisation, irrespective of the quantum, is counterproductive, without the development of the people.

The abundance of the entire area has lured Andhra Pradesh to slowly, steadily and systematically establish control of 21 villages in Kotia Panchayat, of Pottangi. This 'annexation' has not happened overnight. The AP government is doing the following in the area and we are clueless or unfazed:
- Old age pension
- Child Nutrition
- Provision of food security card
- Replacing Odisha with AP as coordinates in Aadhar cards
- Construction of check dam, without informing Odisha government (at Sembi)

- Infrastructure development and road construction to connect the area better to interior AP. (Allocation of budget exceeding Rs 50 Cr.)
- Free food distribution which includes egg, milk and such other daily use items which are required by the households of the panchayat

The civil society of Odisha is in a deep slumber while AP is on an overdrive to snatch away Kotia panchayat from under our nose. The district authorities are not informed about these developments (at least they claim so) and if they are not then that itself should be taken as a major laxity endangering the existence of the habitations and the people. How are we even accepting these ridiculous alibis?

Kotia Panchayat has always been a part of Odisha, as it was in the erstwhile Jeypore estate. During the state formation in 1936, Government of India issued an order which was published in The Gazette of India, on 19th March 1936, vide no. F. 20/35 G(B). This order mentions (in the First Schedule, Part-I, Sl. No. 2(iv)) that the areas under the then new Province of Odisha, shall comprise of "the following areas in the Vizagapatnam district, that is to say, the Jeypore (Impartible) Estate and so much of the Pottangi Taluk as is not included in that estate."

During the formation of Odisha state, which was on linguistic basis, a survey was undertaken in three states – Bihar, MP and Odisha to identify and demarcate the revenue villages and the territories. Surprisingly only seven villages of Kotia Gram Panchayat (Pottangi block), like Turia, Barabandha, Talakanti, Gumelpadara, Mathalamba, Suliamari, and Katraguda were recorded as the revenue villages and since then revenue has been collected by the State. 21 villages are left out as Kotia Gram Panchayat consists of a total of 28 revenue villages. I have spoken to many bureaucrats, local peer leaders and the civil society at large but haven't got any plausible answer to the great *faux pas*. I would like to believe that it was truly, only a faux pas an no inter-state geo-political machination.

Odisha, it seems has woken up to the ingression and has started its activities to instil faith and belongingness in the Kotia Panchayat people in their state and the administration. Last month the area received mobile connectivity, but the internet (data) connectivity so far, is patchy. Surprisingly the connectivity gets activated only when there are official visits or important meetings in the area. I am sure our outreach would improve and be targeted directly at the people who unfortunately feel unmoored. AP is organising community meetings, distributing solar lights, blankets and strengthening its strategic penetration into the Panchayat.

The population of the panchayat area is slightly more than 8100 and Odisha has embarked upon a timeline-based area development plan for the Kotia Panchayat. With an immediate outlay of about Rs 60 Cr the infrastructure at Kotia would be strengthened and that includes roads, bridge, hospital, schools. The deadline for all the work to be completed, in the first phase in 31st March, 2020, which is about three years after the announcement of the government in April 2018 of a special package for Kotia Panchayat development.

The Panchayat should be able to use a 10-bed hospital, a 300-seater hostel for tribal boys and a 200-seater hostel for tribal girls, cluster houses for low income communities under Biju Pucca Ghar Yojana, community centres in 5 villages (as the cluster community hubs), roads in the Panchayat hinterlands and much better connectivity to the panchayat, block and the district headquarters. An inter departmental committee on Kotia GP, chaired by the Chief Administrator, KBK, has been steering the development work.

This is a long pending dispute between the states – Odisha & AP and is sub-judice in Supreme Court since 1968. It is not only about the ownership of 21 of the 28 villages in Kotia panchayat but about territorial rectitude and cohesion in Odisha family – the remote habitat of our tribal siblings. They have to be brought into our fold because there is enough evidence that Kotia Panchayat is in Odisha.

The CC road from Naradavalasa to Kotia, a stretch of 8 kms has been build by AP and another road in Talaganjeipadar is now complete. In the teeth of such aggressive plans to seize the territory, Odisha needs to do the following immediately:

- Employ a hardcore communication drive to sensitise the population about the development work it has undertaken
- Involve community champions to advocate the development of the area
- Develop a systematic way of informing people about the ongoing works in the area
- Employ the local population, as much as possible, in the development works underway

These could be the baby steps in confidence building measures.

AP is driving it's development agenda strongly and quite competitively – when Odisha provides Rs 500 towards pension, they offer four times (about Rs 2000) the amount as pension. They look committed and tenacious in their efforts in owning up the land. Odisha needs to generate and sustain the confidence of the people of the Panchayat in it and it's activities, which have to be needs based. Otherwise we would miss the bus and the inclusion, when it happens, would not be organic. And that in turn would ferment different social and security issues which could disrupt the entire development process of the state. The panchayat is precariously located at the border and amidst rebel lands.

We need to learn from our past blunders in the inclusion of Sareikala and Kharsuan in Odisha and the ensuing fiasco. We have suffered, inexcusably, by losing the territories which were rightfully ours but which we acceded due to arrogance of a few of our leaders and unabashed self interest and lowly intrigues to promote individual political careers. This could be a case study of how leaders fail a nation, even if it happened about seven decades ago.

It is our responsibility to ensure a solid, unfractured civil society for our families living at the border areas and who feel alienated.

What do we celebrate on 1st April, if we don't have our entire family with us?

Is it not inconceivable to realise that we still have to bank on a British map of 1945 to validate our claim over 21 disputed Kotia villages? Why not a google map, for instance? We use this antique map because no survey of the area has been done and till date the local habitants do not possess any *patta* for their landholdings.

Kotia & all border districts, panchayats, villages and communities beckon you.

Odisha 2036

Progress lies not in enhancing what is,
But in advancing toward what will be – Khalil Gibran

"Rising Odisha 2036" is an idea whose time has come. This book is possible due to the unflinching belief of Sidhartha Pradhan, the mentor and producer on behalf of Odia Samaj. Besides being the leader, he has instilled the principal tenet of the book ; optimism. Neutral, fact-based analysis and pragmatic optimism is radical. Optimism is the hard choice, the brave choice and is much needed now, in the face of tumult. This book or the compendium expresses our need to declare what needs to be in the face of what is.

In 2036, Odisha would be celebrating its centenary, being the first state in our country to have been created on the basis of language and has also been much underestimated over the years for it being poor and repeatedly thrown back to the poverty trap by natural disasters. In spite of the reversals or the laggard growth, Odias speak modestly, are piety driven, and practice peace, which Thomas Keating would have called the modern mindfulness or contemplative centring. This scarce life force needs to be sustained and very soon gross happiness index would firmly substitute gross domestic product. But the happiness should be deep rooted in development and development in equitable growth of all sections of the society and all geographies. This compendium "Rising Odisha 2036" is aimed at collating thoughts from all sections of the civil society on the 'democracy of development' which would steer the state of "equanimity" to the super highway of growth by 2036. Rising Odisha 2036 would be the guiding anthology to help trigger talking points in the civil society, often restless to improve Odisha beyond a numerical growth figure – it is about quality of life rather than mere statistics. Odisha could be the pioneer in 'economic nationalism' and be model for others to replicate. In place of intense hard data only, you would find intense analysis by experts from various sectors – agriculture, sports, education, health technology, tourism, tribal, culture, social development, films and many more in this one-of-its kind 'thought stack'. It is certainly not a statistical handbook replete with development gobbledygook. Rather, Rising Odisha 2036 is a sounding board, a civil society roundtable in the shape of a book.

As I am writing these two mountaineers from Odisha – Kusha Arlaba of Koraput and Lipika Seth of Bargarh have scaled Mount Kilimanjaro, the tallest mountain in Africa. They took 5 days to reach a peak of 5895 meters above sea level and hoisted the tri colour. Odisha would not take even a century to demonstrate that a rich heritage can be the propeller to a luminous future. That's the firm belief on which is based this compendium which is futuristic, imaginative and in many ways aspirational.

History, politics, economics, social dynamics have shaped Odisha in a way which is probably not quite akin to many other states of India. Much before the formation of the state, Odisha had international maritime trade with south Asian countries, was the first state to be formed on linguistic grounds without rancour & violence, is the state known for time tested civility of its people despite natural disasters ravaging life frequently. National & international businesses are aware of Odisha's worth in it's rich soil and sub-soil. While the bountiful natural resources and reserves are with the tribals, they are the worst sufferers of apathy in the entire development process. The richest is the poorest. Do we continue like this?

Economic liberalisation need not be only a story of private sector success and continuing struggle by the state to provide decent public goods – basic education, health, police, courts judiciary, roads, safety nets. These public goods enable the poor to catch up with the rich. Many believe that the most equalising form of investment is good education, creating human capital. Human capital is considered even more important than the economic capital. The government education has remained dismal and hence spending more would have no impact on the outcomes. The latest ASER report suggests that school children are close to functional illiteracy. Can we not factor in more creative curriculum in the school education to help build the students' character and allow them more room to give vent to their latent creativity? Why should they still follow the rote education system, which would never benefit them ? We should invest in education and this doesn't imply creating education factories in the name of moribund public education.

What is the law of harvest? The law of harvest is to reap more than you sow. Sow an act, and you reap a habit. Sow a habit, and you reap a character. Sow a character and you reap a destiny - James Allen

The Odia diaspora, across the globe has shown tremendous interest in this compendium. Many of them have contributed on topics quite innovative. They have shown a strong desire in contributing to the development of their place of origin, Odisha. Foreigners and expats have contributed to Rising Odisha 2036. They love Odisha, the seat of "soft power" in India. And they aspire to see a much healthier Odisha in 2036. In fact, many opine that Odisha is comparable to the 20 countries at the bottom of the HDI list of UNDP. Had Odisha been a separate country, then it would have been placed between the Central African Republic and Eritrea at the bottom of the list. They feel that under Human Development Indices, Odisha needs to make sustainable and sincere efforts in addressing Consumption Poverty, Infant Mortality Rate (IMR), Under Five Mortality, Institutional Delivery and Primary Education. The experts feel that there is an urgent requirement to formulate District Specific Development Policies in Odisha as Human Development Index (HDI) in some of the districts is lagging behind. The State Administration need to go for specific Development Policies and Plans for the Districts. Because District Level Planning will help out the backward areas in the State more concretely and also contribute majorly to India's efforts in meeting Sustainable Development Goals (SDGs). Districts like Angul, Sundargarh, Jharsuguda, Khurda and Cuttack have experienced higher level of HDI. But Malkangiri, Koraput, Rayagada, Nabarangpur, Kalahandi, Nuapada and Balangir are the districts still reeling under lower level HDI, after almost two decades of HDI based planning and interventions. Proportion of multidimensional poverty is low in Khordha, Cuttack and Puri where as it is high in Malkangiri, Nabarangpur, and Kalahandi the backward districts need District Specific Planning which would result in substantial improvement in HDI. Odisha is not limited only to Cuttack, Bhubaneswar or Puri. Development needs to be equitable and democratic. Strengthening the Public Health Care system with adequate supply of drugs and diagnostic services is an urgent need and introducing purchasing mechanism (procurement remains a cumbersome process) to enhance efficiency will improve service delivery mechanism. The budget allocation for health is likely to increase by about 11% from Rs 6160 crore in 2018-19. The state by 2036 would be implementing major initiatives to strengthen trauma and emergency care across public and private sectors. Under Ayushman Bharat Scheme, Health and wellness centers will cater to people's primary health care needs. These centers will provide comprehensive healthcare including for non communicable diseases and maternal and child health services. These centers should also be providing free essential drugs and diagnostic services.

We might require and conduct international shows, roadshows, hype and hyperbole. But also need internal socio-economic balance in the same breath. Dongrias of Rayagada have not yet received their due as citizens of the state and are still clueless about development. They are sandwiched between avaricious and capricious interests of the state, industry and the 'mainstream'. How far can we keep them 'deviously' away from basic amenities of life? Nothing changes amidst shrewd data manipulations. No electricity, no water, no food, no dreams for youths, no education and still the shrill of "Happy New Year 2019" in social media. Do you plan to continue in this imbecile way till 2036? A new study to evaluate neonatal and under-five mortality at district level and state level in India, indicates that in Rayagada the mortality rate is 141.7, probably the highest in the country. Kanduru of Malipada using a mobile phone is no indicator of economic growth. Inequality and poverty have not declined for him and his family of 4. The forests are dwindling, the forest dwellers are perishing without any skills, migration of the strong, proud tribal youths is increasing by the day. We are pushing them to the polluted cities, bursting at the seams, struggling with civic amenities and order. Raw and guileless youth energy is being systematically sapped. The state has to take charge. Equity matters for development. It is the soul of development. It is important for its own sake and for higher growth. If personal, rural-urban and regional disparities are reduced, growth will increase. We need to define equity in terms of empowerment and increase in the participation of the poor, so that there will be no trade-off between growth and equity.

Voltaire had said that "Injustice in the end produces independence". I would say, inequality in the end produces independence. Inequality has to perish by 2036, in Odisha.

Major cities of Odisha, Cuttack, Bhubaneswar, Berhampur, Sambalpur with high density of population would go for multi level parking lots to decongest major areas of the cities. Besides roads, footpaths in the market would also be repaired as part of the decongestion process. It is better to have the projects executed on a PPP model Mostly in these cities located next to the main bus stand in the city or the old city, the market is popular because unlike the malls and the supermarkets products there are cheaper and more in variety. There are parking lot for visitors but those remain mostly empty due to poor maintenance or distance from the main hub. Instead visitors park their vehicles wherever they find space, leading to chaos and congestion. The Smart Cities could have digital on-the-spot geotagging attendance system for cops on traffic duty. The high tech system is expected to check attendance related irregularities and ensure that traffic cops are present at their assigned locations, not just on paper. There could be the move to introduce weekly offs for traffic cops to reduce stress. At present traffic inspectors move from one spot to another to take manual attendance of these cops. The system is vulnerable to misuse.

Time is always right to do what is right. – Martin Luther King

As India has finalised an exclusive Rs 5650 Cr military infrastructure development plan spread over 10 years for the strategically located Andaman & Nicobar archipelago, Odisha by 2036, ie. Another 17 years, would be straddled in our defence plan. Odisha would soon be the place for stationing of warships, aircraft drones, missile batteries and infantry soldiers.

Rapid economic growth and the use of technology for social sector programmes would help Odisha make a significant dent in extreme poverty in the state. The idea that creativity is not part of science is quite silly. Science is pretty much a very creative endeavour fuelled by imagination. I hope to see by 2036 much of the misinformation "that scientists are not passionate" to die down. We need to revamp our education system and by 2036 a lot of our teachers would understand that children are born scientists and are curious. That level of curiosity has to be generated and retained.

The Prime Minister of India has given a clarion call:
Jai Jawan Jai Kisan
Jai Vigyan Jai Anusandhan

"The government of India has emphasised on the role of science for building a new and prosperous India by connecting science to society, from school students to scientists, from basic science to technology, from technology to innovation to start-ups, from agriculture to artificial intelligence, from atom to astrophysics and by focusing on our needs and priorities in health, agriculture, food, energy, water, education and transport for the security and prosperity of the nation."

Odisha should take advantage of facilities under National Mission on interdisciplinary Cyber-physical systems, MANAK (Million Minds Augmenting National Aspirations and Knowledge), NIDHI (National Initiative for Developing and harnessing Innovations), KIRAN (Knowledge Involvement in Research Advancement through Nurturing), VIGYAN JYOTI (School Girls enrolment into the top S&T institutions), AWSAR (Augmenting Writing Skills for Articulating Research) and creating international connect. Digitisation has touched every aspect of human life and in Odisha it is expected to alter how organisations look at business sectors, markets, service their customers and ideate new businesses in the next 15-20 years. Digitisation, on which the Prime Minister and the Governments lay emphasis on, can save time and expenses as a panacea, while enhancing their extend and effectiveness. The three-fold transformation of consumers, government and industry would have far reaching economic consequences. The number of technologies evolving, be it the internet of things (IoT), Artificial Intelligence (AI), Robotics would touch every sector, reimagining how goods and services would be delivered, specifically in the logistics sector. This would impact lives in Odisha like never before and would herald what is now being termed as Industry 4.0. I foresee the usage of advanced technologies in Odisha by 2036, specifically in information and telecommunication systems, digital solutions and services, infrastructure systems, industrial systems like water, oil and gas supply and management, to transportation and urban development solutions. Digitisation is radical and it will bring in the much-needed inclusiveness and true social transformation in the complex social dynamics in Odisha.

We hope that by 2036, premium institutes in Odisha would mentor schools located close to their campuses to ensure that students do not lag behind in mathematics and science subjects. It is vital to foster research tendency among students right from the primary schools. Maths can be taught in an entertaining way. For the students to study and understand maths and science properly, not very big equipment's but simple ideas are required. Hence primary school teachers play a big role.

We have been focussing on the macros all these while and while that continues, by 2036, we would also have the micro or the bottom taken care of. Experts suggest that there should be selected districts depending on specific economic criteria and the districts will get special attention in ease of doing business. It is almost a certainty that the $2.6 trillion economy of India will scale the $5 trillion milestone over the next seven – nine years and would touch the $10 trillion mark by the turn of 2035. New industrial policy linking global supply chain is required and would be mutually beneficial by 2036. And the share of Odisha in the national economy should exceed 20 percent. I hope to see an industrial policy in operations, which would be aiming at developing global value chains and boosting Odisha's and hence India's manufacturing competitiveness. There is a need for our industries to tap global supply chains because manufacturing can't happen end to end in one geography. It has to be part of a global value chain and global supply chain. By 2036, Odisha with its hugely improved infrastructure by then, should help India develop mutually beneficial value chain and supply chains. India in 2036 is expected to be one of the largest market economies and would have developed from one of the fastest growing emerging market economies. The nature of attracting investments would also undergo a sea change.

The state, with support from the centre, by 2036 is expected to prepare a list of global companies sitting with huge cash balance and these would be targeted to get investments. The government should be ready with a management appraisal system which should help it make the industrial policy dynamic in view of the changing trends across the world. The world has now realised that manufacturing cannot happen end to end in one geography. It has to be a part of a global value chain and global supply chain. One important aspect of the industrial policy should be the focus on the districts as a part of a bottom up approach for boosting growth. Each district should be responsible as a unit of development and the focus should be on one district at a time and increase its GDP growth by three four percentage points annually, and this in turn would help increase the SGDP and the national GDP. Accordingly, the state by 2036, should identify districts, map their baseline of their economy and will work on specifics to increase their economic output. The measures being undertaken to push growth at district levels are aimed at achieving this high target (of a national $10 trillion economy by 2035-6) earlier. While the country is now targeting to increase the annual FDI inflows to $100 billion, I see a great opportunity for Odisha to augment through the development of its select districts. Odisha has now already been discussed as a focal state/ region for the joint efforts by India and South Korea towards developing a dynamic world trading platform. India is planning to increase the manufacturing GDP to $1 trillion as part of taking its GDP to $5 trillion by 2025 and to $10 trillion by 2030. At a time when global economy is slowing down and India continues to remain a growth spot, it should be Odisha's cooperative endeavour to make Indian economy grow and hence world economy grow for which partnerships and mutually rewarding relationships are essential.

It is necessary for Odisha to increase its focus on services and merchandise exports. A vibrant capital market is essential both for mobilising capital as well as make it work effectively such that it delivers maximum returns for the economy. And we as part of the civil society of Odisha should be an integral part of the planning and execution process.

Farmers (and crops) without borders is the future of food and a strong agricultural sector in Odisha should be transparent, adaptable and unified, and it should recognize that many of the crops we grow today might have originated elsewhere. Agricultural sectors around the world are sharing information like never before. Hence the perfect variety of seed these days will likely contain traits from China, India, Argentina and more. Odisha has not been accentuating long term structural changes which would make agriculture more profitable, sustainable and resilient. We must increase the resilience of our agriculture and make it a much more rewarding profession for our farmers. A few short terms schemes and doles would not help the agriculturists. By 2036 we expect to have stable farm packages to tackle the debt crisis in the agriculture sector amid projected reversals with a spate of farm loan waivers and rising distress in the sector. Agriculture should be our prime focus, in Odisha even in 2036 as it is the backbone of our economy and is the primary source of livelihood for over 60 percent of the population. The civil society hopes to see farmers diversify into allied activities like poultry, horticulture and fishing to ensure sustainable livelihoods. With value addition our food processing industry and horticulture should have immense scope for expanding its footprints. We should focus on home grown food security for all, more investment, crop diversification and value addition. With population increasing regularly, Odisha cannot sustain on imported food security. By 2036 more farmers would resort to organic methods of farming and practice and promote the judicious use of inputs and irrigation.

Climate change is already staring, and its effects are being felt with increasing force and intensity. It is no longer about some distant future and decisions made today will impact us in our near future. Odisha, hopefully will invest billions of dollars in public infrastructure over the next few years. Conducive policies should also aim to massively increase private investments across sectors – manufacturing, services and agriculture. Each of these policies and investments will have time horizons spanning five to 50 years. There is currently no formal process by which projects of a certain scale would have to go through a risk assessment and a cost-benefit analysis of the potential impact of climate change related effects. Ordinary citizens too are directly experiencing climate uncertainty in their lives, especially from extreme events.

One could go on. But let's read the brilliant minds who have made efforts to write for Rising Odisha 2036.

We are determined to rise.

Sailing away...

(An adaptation of Akshaya Mohanty's *Ja Re Bhasi Bhasi Ja* on canvas)

Meandering river
Blue waves slithering,
Lissome maiden,
Nimble-footed on the stone
Lighting every creek,
With her coy outpour
On life's gondola
Through the curvy path
Meandering river

Every nymphet has a story and so does every bend in the river – well juxtaposed. As the boater oars along Mahanadi the maiden at every anchor has something to tell him. Who else can she confide in?

The waterman is her friend for the moment because the next moment he is gone along the flow. That's the flow of life. Today here, not there tomorrow. "Out beyond ideas of wrongdoing and rightdoing there is a field. I'll meet you there. When the soul lies down in that grass the world is too full to talk about." That's where she needs a moment, your moment Oh Sailor. She has so many emotions to share, so many family wires which would design her future life. Has anyone ever asked, what she wants? Her life partner is to be decided by others, excluding her.

This ballad, first of its kind in Odia, became a chart buster and remains a cult narration of geographies, demographies and their specificities. A treatise on middle class, Odia family caught between groom hunting for their daughter, the struggle of catering to the new capital Bhubaneswar's clerk groom's 'demand', the helplessness of dark complexioned girl and the confidence of a Cuttacki girl, ready to face the world on her own terms.

At every curve on the canvas, I meet the beauty (because for me the sailor, a maiden is a maiden is a maiden) as a confidante and a gypsy listener. Someone is needed to listen to her. She has a voice. At home everyone is busy crafting her life except herself. But this doesn't dampen her spirits – she is still aware of her beauty, the need to preserve her 'demure'. Her gaze is straight and her conversation uncharacteristically confident.

Only Akshaya Mohanty could pen this, compose this with all the elements of folk tune and still make it popular and not pedantic or boring. Lines like "Majuchi suna diha"- scrubbing the golden body, colours it 'flirtatious' or 'cheeky'. That's refreshingly natural and ahead of its time for the prudish seventies.

I can see the ballad on the canvas – the boat trudging along the slithering small waves of the big river (Mahanadi), anchoring at Sambalpur, Kantilo, Banki, Cuttack and downstream with a palette of white and blue, lines of thick tresses of hair basking on the bathing stones, sheer uninhibition of the lolita at every creek. The protagonists are three or four and the story is lively enough to be captured in the canvas.

Truly, life and romance begin with water and taper with water, the boatman being the mute witness, till he calls out to his friend at the other shore. I miss *nauria daka* (the shout out of the boatman). There is no water and there is no witness.

■

Odisha Budget: Climate Change

Odisha's population in 2020 would be approximately 4.8 Cr and is slated to rise much faster in the coming 2-3 years due to rapid industrialisation, spurt in mining activities and infrastructure projects and development activities. Today Odisha is one of the fastest growing states in India and I foresee a reverse migration situation in the not-so-far future. The trends would signal in the next 6 months.

This is time to put into action programs to balance environment concerns and development. to achieve development objectives of ensuring food security, creating jobs, reducing poverty and improving health. A major deterrent would be the impending natural disasters. Odisha is sitting on a climate emergency. Rising temperatures in Bay of Bengal, growing incidence and intensity of extreme weather events, the threat of extinction of at least half a million species, the destruction of forests, and the disruption of ecosystem services would directly hit the economic activities.

We are still traumatised by FANI, the powerful

cyclone which hit Odisha and had left a trail of destruction which has ravaged lives, destroyed families and livelihoods. Odisha region has experienced the landfall of at least four major cyclones in the last two decades which have indurated the people. Super cyclone of 1999, Phailin of 2013, Hud Hud of 2014, Titli of 2018, the blizzard of disasters, has spelt unimaginable disaster for the state and the country. A study says that the number of extremely hot days in the state would increase by 30 times from 1.62 in 2010 to 48.05 by 2100. The desertification and water shortage would severely cripple our agrarian economy which translated to numbers mean 30% of the Net State Domestic product (NSDP) and about 75 percent of employment (the work force engaged in this sector). The GDP per capita of [1] 92,727 would slide down by about 15 percent due to disaster striking again this FY.

Lord Jagannath forbid. But every family has provision for contingency, and we should budget for the same for Odisha.

Investments in ecological infrastructure are imminent. Renewable energy-based electricity, improved watershed conservation and forest management and green jobs are some of the environmental interventions strongly suggested. These interventions can help in stable incomes and support safe livelihoods. DMF (Rs 4,453 crore in four years, of which about half the money is spent) , CAMPA (In 19-20 a provision of Rs 592.52 crore CAMPA annual plan was made and this FY it should be increased by at least 20% , to Rs 660 Cr because the area to be covered would be more, about 20%) & CSR funds put together would not exceed Rs 3500 Cr for deployment in 20-21.

In 2020 the World Economic Forum ranked climate change as the biggest risk to economy and society. An inference from a Stanford University study raises the possibility of Odisha GDP going down by about 10% as a result of the warming climate and the recurrence of disaster which is predicted. Odisha's average summer temperature, a study establishes, will be far higher than the national average increase from about 24 degree Celsius to about 28 degree Celsius, which means that we need to brace up for much harsher climatic conditions and more deaths and morbidities. This would directly eat into the GDP and the economic growth.

Odisha has pioneered sector-wise development programs to for climate-vulnerable people, specifically women and children. Fish Pond Yojana and Banayana project for women almost always at the receiving end of the climate emergency and livelihoods programs for small and marginal farmers (landholdings less than 1 hectare). But the budgetary provision is required to either factor these programs or elements into the existing livelihoods verticals or create separate programs under the direct supervision of the district Collector. About Rs 3000-4000 Cr is required (additionally) for livelihoods support to communities at risk. The climate induced disasters strike anywhere, not restricted to only the coastal areas. The impact of carbon emissions is going to be more pronounced in Odisha in the coming years.

Odisha is the climate-constrained state that we will have to be constantly aware of and the state Budget 2020 is aimed at propelling us to a $1 trillion economy. Investments would be severely eroded if we do not mitigate climate related damages. The civil society is urged to allocate sizeable amount of next year's budget to measures to address climate change. Not only welfare programs but climate-related spending on innovation, research and infrastructure need to be taken up in the state on urgent basis.

We can bring in investments, plan mega projects, provide comprehensive social securities, build professional institutions but one stroke of disaster would swamp us to nought. Nothing else matters but a safe living and sustainable livelihood. The budget has to incorporate climate emergency management.

■

Sarbeswar, the born crusader

Sarbeswar Mohapatra, the young and dynamic social reformer of Odisha is no more. He passed away at Ambapua, Ganjam last night after a massive cardiac arrest. Many in their condolence messages reiterate that At 49 and with his passion for social change he had many more plans to help Odisha change and sustain. His death is a severe loss to the development sector of Odisha. Mr Mohapatra was the regional Director of FIDR and the Founder of Nirmata. He has been actively involved in pioneering Technology for Good in the state. Since over last 20 years he has been giving a lot of his time to the primary education and child rights in the state and specifically in Ganjam.

A proud son of the soil, he has been awarded with many prestigious recognitions for his contribution to making the society a better place to live. In the early 2000 he emerged as a leading social activist who took upon himself the task of reaching out to households in HIV/AIDS awareness, working with self help groups (SHGs) wives of migrant workers. Just a day before his death he was leading the management of migrant workers in his area by counselling them and helping them with food and other socio-psychological support. With his efforts Ganjam has been successful in eliminating child labour (he represented Childline) to a large extent and he was known for his exemplary work in rescuing children from eateries and other business establishments. Sarbeswar Bhai as he was popularly known, has been supporting the government in its efforts in enforcing the Child Labour (Prohibition and Regulation) Act and giving back dignity to the children and the families.

A tireless reformer, he has worked considerably in the Urban Slum program across Odisha including in Khariar NAC of Nuapada district, Konark and other places to help provide land rights to the slum dwellers under the Odisha land Right to Slum Dwellers Act 2017.

He was a known peace activist who was invariably called upon to resolve community, social and family issues. Because of his sincerity, idealism and discipline, he was revered in the communities and was always the "go to Guru". An ardent Sai devotee, he spoke to the communities regularly on moral stories and spiritualism and hence contributed tremendously to the peace and harmony in the areas. He was always available, round the clock, to help anyone wanting support – from a child to senior citizens, his door was always open for everyone. Many in the community had unflinching faith in his spiritual guidance. Constantly moving from village to village he had rescued a new born, abandoned baby On 22nd May and had taken the entire responsibility of admitting the baby at MKCG Hospital Berhampur and even signing as guardian to put the baby in ICU and medical procedures.

He would be largely remembered as the social change leader who led by example and developed volunteerism as a powerful way for the youths to gain a strong sense of civic engagement and bring about positive transformational change in their communities. He worked all his life on development themes like social exclusion, lack of rights, gender-based violence, poverty with the help of community work with a deep sense of belongingness and people to people contact. He belonged to everyone in the community and everyone belonged to him.

A true social advocate, he was not limited to rhetoric. Sarbeswar Bhai did bring in social change in some of the most difficult circumstances.

He belonged to the fast disappearing breed of social advocates who dedicated their lives full time to community work, working on-the-ground, house to house. Selfless, Sarbeswar, who worked closely with Mr Charudutta Panigrahi would be remembered forever as the Karmveer who till his last belonged to everyone (sarba eeswar) and would remain the Ganjam Gaurav.

May we have more Sarbeswars, the brave hearts and large hearts of Odisha.

FIDR will observe 31 May as Samuha Divas !

(As expressed and written by the community)

The future of start-ups in Odisha

Start-up is essentially starting up on a new idea. But how do we know that the idea is new or in other words if there is no novelty or value add, then the feasibility of the idea to be rolled out comes under a cloud. In 90s when I started to work, the most common type of start-up company was a dotcom. Venture capital was easy to obtain during that time due to a frenzy among investors to put money on the emergence of these new types of businesses. Unfortunately, most of these Internet start-ups eventually went bust due to major oversights in their underlying business plans, such as lack of sustainable revenue. But even then, Internet start-ups survived when the dotcom bubble burst. Amazon.com and eBay are examples of such companies. Other household names that came later are Facebook, Airbnb, Uber & SpaceX.

But when there is no defined trend and the young entrepreneur has an idea (targeted at providing a solution), it needs to be tested or in the first place be evaluated. The germination of the idea has to be in synchronisation and if that happens then the starting is on a firmer ground and is almost guaranteed to attract larger funding in due course. The gestation period for 'proof of concept' goes down and is a win-win for all. Start-ups need to invest time and money in research. Market research gives the most important insight into the demand for a product or service. And subsequently the start-up requires a comprehensive business plan outlining mission statement, future visions, and goals as well as management and marketing strategies.

But who is going to provide all this support?

Odisha today has about 140 (15%+ are almost defunct) engineering colleges out of which 20 are government institutions. Not limited to engineering colleges alone, Start-up is the vehicle which would transform Odisha from its traditional mindset on education to the new age demand for more applications of education and not theoretical. Application makes all the difference. It is almost justifying the studies or the empirical theories. I was recently speaking at a Start Up panel discussion and Prashant of Start Up Odisha mentioned that there are about 560 start ups registered (rather started) in the last 30 months. This is impressive and more assuring is the target-based drive with a timeline. With these efforts we rank 76th among a total of 143 economies, as per the Global Innovation Index (GII) in Innovation and R&D. In Odisha Start Up is at its nascent stage. Barring about 10 colleges, Start Ups are not pursued vigorously as they should have been. The autonomous universities are also quite dormant in this. There is lot more to do. In Odisha there is 'everything' that can be done ranging from the digital/ technology sector to a wide array of sectors including agriculture, manufacturing, social sector, healthcare, education. In the state there are 35.88 lakh youth in the age-group of 18-23 years, who are not in the higher education system. Odisha's total youths enrolled in higher education is 2.7 per cent of total youths enrolled nationally. The state's Gross Enrolment Rate (GER) in higher education has increased marginally to 22.1 per cent in 2018-19 It was 22 per cent in 2017-18 and 16 per cent in 2010-11. The GER for Scheduled Castes (SC) improved to 20 per cent in 2018-19 from 18.8 per cent in 2017-18. The GER had remained stagnant for the Scheduled Tribes (ST) in the State. It improved to 12.8 per cent in 2018-19 from 12.5 per cent in 2017-18. The GER of Odisha is poorest among the major states of India and this means that that the enrolment of a specific age-group (18-23) is low in Odisha. I believe that this is the time to introduce campus entrepreneurship to the students to make the education smart, attractive and useful for early earning. This would ask for more engagement of colleges in the start-up initiatives of Odisha. In the next 5 years at least 5 hubs should be set up and invigorated at Angul, Rayagada, Berhampur, Rourkela, Jharsuguda. Youth in the emerging tier 2 and tier 3 cities including semi-urban and rural areas which are industrially active, need support and handholding. The start-up drive in Odisha needs to be simplified and demystified. The youth need handholding in ideating, funds support and Industry-Academia Partnership and Incubation. The rapid industrialisation efforts of Odisha would bear fruit in an investment of more than Rs 2,10,000 crore ($30Bn) in sectors like IT, fertiliser, petro chemicals, food processing, health, infrastructure, ESDM, metal and minerals, manufacturing, textiles and tourism. In the next wave of industrialisation in Odisha, the state is expected to shift away from the bracket of being a "Mines and Minerals" state. This shift is necessary to result in proper harnessing of 'rental economy' to add value to the other sectors which are always more sustainable. This should augur well for the "Start Up" movement because industrialisation would spur the need for impact investing in innovations and R&D. In the above Start-up hubs which I have mentioned, I would bat for the CSR of the industries to specifically allocate resources & infrastructure for campus entrepreneurship and innovations. The young innovators need enabling climate to develop their ideas and make them market able. This would help in solving the unemployment challenge for the state. Going forward, with the dominance of AI and machine learning, the present skills would fast become obsolete and we need the next generation to brace up with the help of Start Ups. They should be solution providers, rather than process managers. Interestingly, the State's youth population accounted for around 3.2 per cent of that of the country and mostly live in smaller places.

The All India Council of Technical Education (AICTE) has already done it and the State should also encourage engineering colleges and technical institutions to allow student entrepreneurs to sit for examination even if their attendance is short. The colleges have also been asked to explore provisions of on-campus accommodation to student entrepreneurs and permitting semester break for working on their start-ups. This decision and proactive step would encourage more students to take up research and innovation to turn into entrepreneurs and build a culture of ultimately becoming job givers than job seekers. The colleges/ institutions should allow their students to take a semester or year break (like they can do in other countries) depending upon the decision of a review committee constituted by the institute to work on their start-ups. I strongly support the idea that student entrepreneurs should be allowed to earn academic credits for their efforts while creating an enterprise. Depending on the success of the enterprise the college should give appropriate credits for academics. Some of the lifechanging campus start-ups that went on to become big companies are Notemybook, Practo, Dolojo.

In the next 5 years Odisha should vigorously develop its start up space. This is because if the state has opened itself to mining and extraction industry, it means that the tribal, backward districts would see more disposable income in the near future. I hope so because employment should rise in the semi-skilled and unskilled sectors. If the parents can send their children to colleges and the extraction industries (includes miners, downstream industries, upstream industries, MSME) can support the colleges to develop Start Up as a key thrust area then we could have the students emerge as entrepreneurs and would be absorbed in the eco system of industrialisation in Odisha. It would be a complete picture. Otherwise migration of our youth to the metros would continue unabated resulting in the exodus one whole generation from the state. ICT & Wireless technology, Pharma & healthcare, manufacturing technologies, water technologies, material energy are some of the areas which demands more innovations and R&D. India as a country is struggling with R&D.

By 2024-5, Odisha should have one of the highest numbers of MSMEs in India. Hence there would be more opportunities for Start-ups, both in terms of business development, funds support and incubation. But in colleges we need the teachers or the Start-up cells (which is essential to be created in the campuses) to be able to train entrepreneurs and wanna-be entrepreneurs and give them the confidence they need to succeed and to grow their businesses. Start-up training should vary according to the stage of development of a business and should not be a "one-size fits all". It should include peer learning, sharing knowledge and know-how, and mentoring. That is why the teachers in colleges need Start up orientation and trainings. They should mentor the participants to generate ideas, prepare business plans and propel their businesses to the next level. Part of this process means providing training support for those considering entrepreneurship as a career, through to business start-up, business growth and sustainability. So, a solid Train the trainers program should be started now so that in one calendar year we would have a definite number of trainers ready to groom start-ups in their colleges. The district Industry office or the IPO would have to play a major catalytic role in this process.

It would be a social change program, if the start-up drive in Odisha provides a vital step in getting young people to start their own businesses and in tribal areas develop their business ideas, get access to finance and build networks, making them more likely to succeed in the coming 5 years. I can't see beyond 5 years now, because we have so much to do at colleges in Aska, Bhawanipatna, Koraput, Khariar, Deogarh, Baripada, and everywhere. Let the civil society be involved in the Start Up movement and not be a silent spectator to a life changer.

Start-ups can make Odisha the **Idea Centrepoint of India**.

Rangabati and much beyond

I can't imagine Odisha being a breakthrough state and a $1 trillion economy without harnessing the rich west Odisha. Western part of Odisha has deep seated cultural identity, rootedness coupled with rich natural resources for manufacturing sector and veritable traditional agriculture practices. Bargarh possesses everything from Nrusinghnath to Rice to Fashion. It is one of those zones in India, which in the next decade should together contribute to more than half of the country's GDP. It is good news that paddy cultivation land parcel has increased to 62,815 hectares (ha), this rabi season and production pegged at about 3,95,735 MT and more. Other crops including paddy, pulses, oilseeds, vegetable, condiments and sugarcane are being cultivated in about 1,30,000 ha. But the water management in command areas during the current crop season remains inefficient. Cotton plantation is healthy in Balangir. Patnagarh is the cotton belt of Balangir district and produces good quality cotton. But unpredictable weather conditions last year (during this time: September and October) had a severely adverse impact on the crop. Untimely rain and cloudy conditions affect the crop adversely as either "boll bursting" does not occur or the bolls turn black. This year there has been fall in the number of bolls for each plant. Cotton growers should not migrate in search of labour. In the 8.4 pc growth of Odisha in 2018-19, the share of agriculture sector is declining giving away space to service and manufacturing in that order. This trend, if we allow to continue would harmfully affect the income level of the agrarian families (70% of the state) dependant on agriculture. The small farmers, cultivators and landless agricultural labourers would be benefitted by the KALIA scheme but sustenance of farming as a practice is in question. There are about 260000 farming families in the district out of which about 80% are small and marginal farmers. They survive in spite of a meagre 11 % and 5 % of total cultivated area touched by the irrigation system during Kharif and Rabi seasons. To enhance irrigation potential and public investment in the agriculture sector, the state has allocated about 9,216 crore in 2017-18 but it is time to assess the impact in the agriculture intensive districts of western Odisha.

Most of the districts follow a single cropping pattern and the capacities of the farmers need to be built in crop diversity. The DPMU in each district should be primarily responsible for preparing the district plans. I have not seen most of the plans.

While most of the districts are agrarian, Jharsuguda is an industrial hub. About 35 panchayats are mining affected and forest cover is only 10 % and net sown area is about 43%. Acute Respiratory Infection, Tuberculosis (TB), Diabetes, Diarrhoea/Dysentery result in high morbidities in the district. DMF lie underutilised, keeping the high priority sector projects wanting. Drinking water, education, environment preservation, pollution control, health and sanitation, skill development and livelihood activities need immediate attention. In 2017, An agreement to undertake Project Monitoring Unit (PMU) for the District Mineral Foundation (DMF) Jharsuguda was signed between the district administration and a big four consulting firm. But DMF allocation has not shown expected improvement in efficiencies. Jharsuguda's contribution to the state economy is dominant. The placement to live register ratio in youth employment is shockingly low. Are the local youths properly trained? If yes, then why are they not getting locally employed? In Jharsuguda, they should all be absorbed in industry-centric jobs. Otherwise I don't see any point in local growth which is sustainable. CSR programs so far have been glossy stories for annual reports, not practical handholding for the hapless youth.

Nuapada's listing as the second top 'Most Improved Districts' of the country in 'Improvement in Education' category is good news but migration for labour continues to plague the district. To prevent distress migration, the State has worked out an Integrated Action Plan (IAP) to pilot in 30 GPs of thee blocks in two districts, Balangir and Nuapada (Belpada and Khaprakhol in Bolangir district and Nuapada in Nuapada district). Around 8,433 households in two blocks of Balangir district and 719 HHs in Nuapada block of Nuapada district have been identified as vulnerable to migration. I am not sure how this 'identification' has been done. But it is common sense that the family details, land holding patterns, livelihood options and skill maps of these households should have been surveyed. Intersectoral linkages is a must for all the relevant departments to pitch in collaboratively and schemes to be stitched together to see impact on the ground. Agro forestry, poultry, horticulture, micro-irrigation, millet mission, dug well and distribution of pump set and sprinklers, are some of the interventions which can strengthen livelihoods.

In the beginning of 2019, the state had taken up 11,434 projects worth over Rs 6,438.23 crore under District Mineral Foundation (DMF) in various districts – including Jharsuguda and Sundergarh which are in western part of the state and are top contributors (Sundargarh about 800 crore, Jharsuguda about 300 crore). There is no reason why a social audit should not be undertaken, suo motto by the civil society organisations to monitor and help the state in the development of these projects – which included the high priority 9,044 projects like drinking water, education, environment preservation, pollution control, health and sanitation, skill development and livelihoods. But where is the civil society movement in western Odisha? Jharsuguda had 508 projects and Sundergarh 4631 and are in need of socio-technical support.

Last year Kalahandi was adjudged the most improved district in agriculture in India amongst the Aspirational Districts in agriculture sector. Kalahandi is the turnaround story of India and like India. The blot of hunger has driven farmers to try out new varieties and come out of the poverty cycle. Remarkable is the tenacity of the local farming community in Kalahandi. They need technical support - in reducing extensive use of synthetic fertilisers, pesticides and high yielding mono-crop, to arrest the loss of crop varieties, erosion of genetic diversity and stop the extinction of local seeds in the region. The agriculture extension services need to be much more up-to-date. This year Kalahandi farmers are left with an excess of 25,000 quintal paddy unsold. Last season they they faced both flood and drought and are now surviving with water crisis and pest attack. I would continue writing about the other districts in western Odisha.

But what about the civil society and the political leadership in western Odisha? I am not aware of the role the WODC is playing in socio economic development of the region. The political leadership, cutting across party lines are busy positioning as 'state leaders' rather than 'people leaders'. True development starts at the ground. The civil society organisations are busy implementing 'project'. We need programs and not short lived interventions which die before they start.

On Nuakhai , one of the most important festivals in Western Odisha, celebrating fresh harvest, let's go back to the fields. Agriculture needs infusion of technology and smart market linkages. There is no reason why we should not prevent the demise of agriculture, specifically in western Odisha. Islands of success, smart pilots are good to cite but why aren't they replicated?

Nuakhai celebration dates back to the 12th century, encouraged by the king Raja Ramai Deo. The King believed that agriculture was an important activity or vocation which helped in strengthening the societal bonding.

Let's join hearts and celebrate Nuakhai, but not to be blind to the fields and their mentors.

"Change your opinions, keep to your principles; change your leaves, keep intact your roots."

Odisha's biggest gamble

Odisha is opening its treasure vault (ratna bhandara). Don't bracket the author as an anti-mining activist just because I'm trying to break the slumber of the civil society. These thoughts are without an iota of politics.

Rapidity in development was probably never this fierce. The state government in its 5th term, the central government in its 2nd term and Odisha embarking on the gambit to auction mines before their leases expire in March 2020. The treasury of the house is in the marketplace. Almost 25% of the country's iron and manganese ore resources will be up for sale for captive users and merchant miners. By doing so Odisha, the projected steel capital of India would be the principal provider to India's targeted 300mt steel capacity by 2030. Odisha's mines have a direct influence on the economy of India and world trade. With the help of Odisha mines, steel production in India is forecasted to be doubled by 2031, which would contribute about 2.1% to the GDP of the nation and in the next decade its share should be exceeding 3%. The soil of Odisha holds the key to the development of the nation. This is only about the steel sector and there are other minerals from Odisha mines which would transform India's economy forever. Our target is to grow annually at 12% over the next 5 years to a $5 trillion GDP by 2024 and Odisha would play a significantly dominant role in this unprecedented growth story.

But mining so far has not yielded commensurate dividends to the life in the state, if not more. The intoxication of easy money through a rent seeking behaviour is abnormally binding but shockingly short lived. In the past three decades, less than 1% of Odisha has enjoyed abnormal affluence without creating new wealth. The 'rent seeking' addiction is of manic proportions. The richest state of India (the mineral rich state accounting for 7 per cent of India's forests and 11 per cent of its surface water) has been bled poor by only a few in the extraction industry and brazen crony capitalism that includes rampant illegal miners. In rural Odisha, the average value of assets people have is estimated at Rs 2.81 lakh — which is lowest in the country and even in urban, people having an average value of assets of Rs 7.9 lakh, is the poorest. If at all, tinkering with our naturally gifted resources, should be for a purpose for the state. Odisha's civil society is clueless, silent and stunned. Apathy towards own state's development is always worse than flagrant loot of the resources.

Under the soil, Odisha is *ratna bhandara* (treasury of gems), and over the soil Odisha is a perennial struggler. With the opening of the mines, the mining revenue is estimated to cross Rs 12,000 crore, 2021 onwards.

In spite of being the biggest mineral storehouse of India and one of the largest in south Asia, the state today is reeling under an unemployment rate of 7.1 per cent which is more than the national average of 6.1 per cent. GSDP growth by 8.4 per cent is largely due to the industries sector whose share has been consistently rising in the past four years and expected to contribute 39.47 per cent to the Gross State Value Added (GSVA) in 2018-19. Extraction industry accounts for over 30 per cent of the industry's contribution. But with high unemployment, Odisha's youths and households are not benefitted. Agriculture production is sharply declining. Education and agriculture term loans have the highest NPAs in the state. With the revenue from mining, the state should build parallel resources as standby. In about 5 decades from now all our reserves would be depleted and we would be an empty drum, ravaged and dumped.

I am all for mining but responsible mining. Odisha is probably one of the best examples in the world of how non-renewable natural resources are disproportionately important to poor and fragile economies, as typically they are their main endowment and revenue source.

Mine auction is meant for fair play among bidders without any geographical barriers or hegemonies. But this would not necessarily encourage any 'local' entrepreneurs who do not demonstrate investing capabilities at large scale. They are limited in their funds. We are inviting mining behemoths & conglomerates to dig gold, truck and build empires. In the last three decades, only about 80 young people have joined the mining/extraction industry independently (not as scion of established mining families) as mining and allied entrepreneurs and have sustained. Less than 10 mining companies belong to homegrown entrepreneurs. All the rest, numbering 6 times the figure, do not belong to Odisha. Can the government of Odisha provide special incentives for the homegrown businesses? The only trades (and not industries) that mining has spurred over the years are automobile, rentals, logistics, hospitality (low end) and brokering. Odia youths are not present either in the upstream or downstream of mining either as entrepreneurs or employees. The students of Odisha, professionally qualified are not employed with the mining conglomerates due to various reasons. Of the total skilled & semi-skilled workforce less than 12% are Odisha domiciles. There is a skill gap and there is also an opportunity gap. I can see the implosion waiting to happen.

Odisha is at the bottom in the health index score. All the mineral-rich districts of the state are featured in the list of most backward districts of the country. In Keonjhar, the epicentre of mining , 62 per cent of the population lives below poverty line. In Koraput, Asia's bauxite capital, 79 per cent live below poverty line. The income from mineral extraction has not benefitted the regions from where the minerals are removed. Rather poverty has increased. This has majorly affected the social fabric owing to quick gains due to the 'middlemen' syndrome. Only 10 districts get CSR funds deployed (as per the perception of the CSR teams and not as per the needs of the communities assessed) more as tokenism. Has the civil society of Odisha cared to conduct any social audit or impact measurement of these programs? This is no blame game. As a part of the civil society, I take responsibility of having failed in driving development in my state.

The primary health centers could have been managed by these companies to tackle doctors' absence, infrastructural shortcomings but they are not. Odisha has been a pioneer in non-government management of PHCs (with a policy made as early as 2004-5). But CSR funds are 'directed' to be spent in specific agenda. The CAMPA and DMF funds are lying unused.

After the auction of the mines and the

commencement of mining, Odisha's time would be ticking. Every day there would be depletion of natural endowment. Do we watch this, helpless or build alternate, complimentary strengths?

The auctions are being pursued by all the governments with unimaginable alacrity. If this speed and interest could have been used prudently in other sectors too, Odisha would have been the leading example in the world now, of a low-income economy aiming at equitable growth in spite of being a victim of climate emergency and of a legacy of intergenerational poverty.

We have missed the bus in the past, but we are not late. Even now we can make Odisha an island of development by using mining judiciously and smartly, with legitimate Odia nationalism and development in heart. It seems that Odia nationalism and Odisha's wealth are racing in the fast lane of self-destruction.

Let's take three baby steps:

· Let the mining department make public, the area development plans of the competing mining companies. This must (made mandatory) include the plans to mitigate Climate Emergency that Odisha is inevitably, a sitting duck.

· Let the communities (and specifically the PVTGs) be sensitised about the future of their lands and the future their lives in lieu of their donations (they are now made to donate their goldmines to something which they are not aware of)

· Let us have Gram Sabhas on the area development plans of the mining companies and have social approvals of the plans. The social approvals should be devoid of any politics.

Let Odisha leverage the supportive provisions laid

down by the policies and be a global best practice of 'responsible mining'.

This is Odisha's biggest gamble and would make or break the state in no time.

Let's wake up & take care of our home.

Rumi in Konark

The other day I was at Konark and I did both, moon bathing and sun bathing. Moon bathing under the clear blue sky, next to the epitome of tantra, Konark. I realized I am a nothing. Not a thing at all. I keep changing all the time and this metamorphosis from one way to the other is a flow like water. Simple flowing and if there is a block somewhere, it renders me dysfunctional. That's the reason why I stumble, get inefficient, downslide on my performance and belittle my existence. That is where I get small. Only change is unchanging; everything else changes except change. That means only change has eternity. It is a continuum. I danced under the smiling, romantic moon. Far away was the whistling wood, the gentle breeze caressing the Jhaun trees eternally. They always do that whether I am there or not. The waves dash the sand in white lines, waxing under the moon whether I am there or not. Time does not wait. We have to go on, we have to change, because change is the only constant. Konark has also changed. Since the 13th century, there have been waves of change all around. The splendor has changed. But under the same moon, Konark still croons with the waves. Still longs for a little love. Love is certainly not defacing the walls of the chariot with plaster which is faceless. In the godly environs of Chandrabhaga, I could hear the wailing danseuses. No one looks at them before or after "festivals", which is almost parading them. They long passionate love in solitude and not "mean" cacophony.

"There is a candle in your heart, ready to be kindled.
There is a void in your soul, ready to be filled.
You feel it, don't you?"
Rumi

Today there is void in Konark. We have to fill with life. I feel a pulsating, dynamic Tantra at Konark. It is alchemy; it can transform our centers, it can transform the others' centers, it can create a rhythm and harmony between us and our beloved. This is the beauty of Tantra. The precious Tantra at Konark gives us the science of transforming ordinary lovers into soul mates. And that is the grandeur of Konark. It can transform the whole earth; it can transform each couple into soul mates. Each partnership transformed is the great revolution we are looking forward to. We want to live as smart human beings, shackles-free, beautiful, momentous, radiating, and strong. Konark is our navigator, the laboratory, the science of beauty.

"I want to sing like the birds sing, not worrying about who hears or what they think." Rumi

Truly blessed is the land that has Konark. It is the culmination of thoughts, ahead of their times. The chariot of artistes' perception which knows no bounds, leaping ahead. Seamless is the imagination and this is the place where imagination has touched the divine. This divinity of human form is what I believe is tantra.

No wonder it is an obeisance to the Sun God. The life creator. Early morning I was at the altar with the first ray of the Sun kissing the stone sanctorum. When I stood there at the top bowing to the might and tender love of creation, I was marveling at my birth as a human being. This is worship for me. Worshipping the world and the "beyond". Do you think after this orgasmic shake up, I would continue to be the same human, frittering away days, months, years, not prostratting to the Supreme all around us: the trees, the birds, the sky, the waves. Why do I disable my life years deliberately and still be foolish to assume that I am smart. Konark humbles you. It is elixir; it is the pinnacle of dexterity, unfettered and the ultimate evidence of pragmatism. It told me that nothing is impossible. Possibility is what is has demonstrated. Yet I while away my time, drowned in mediocrity. Konark is the colossus of timeless brilliance. Times change, life is change. Konark is the watcher. It is the tantric.

Heraclitus had said: You cannot step in the same river twice. Life, the river, is constantly moving. We know this but treat ourselves as the mosssmudged stagnant rocks. Twelve hundred years ago lived Mevlana Rumi, the eclectic, great sufi mystic poet. His words are essentially sources of deep silences, echoes of inner and the innermost songs. He was not life-negative, but life-affirmative. And the meditation that he has found has been based on the whirling dance which has continued for seven hundred years among mystics. His followers are called whirling Sufis or dervishes. When he did whirling himself, he realized that if you go on whirling there comes a moment when the center of your being remains static and your whole body, mind, brain, everything, whirls. And that center which does not whirl, is you, the center of the cyclone. The whirling is almost like a cyclone, but exactly in the middle of the cyclone/the eye, you will find a point which has not moved at all. Every wheel needs a center on which to turn, and the center has to remain fixed. He tried whirling for thirty six hours, not stop and then discovered the enlightenment like an electric current. Absolutely dazzling, quivering. This center of cyclone is what I felt at Konark. The center having seen, experienced, watched many a storm. And has not lost the sheen, the glory, the self-respect.

This is our heritage: rare in humanity, ahead of its time, resplendent in glory, eclectic, transforming and dynamic.

Why be suicidal?

Primary school dropouts in Rayagada District

Rayagada district has the maximum (11.67%) dropout rate in Odisha, at the primary school level. I, as a part of the civil society, take responsibility for this reprehensible outcome of primary education.

There are 11 Block Education Officers (BEO) who have replaced the DI schools, and each BEO is in charge of education in the block. Under each BEO there are about 25 people working in various capacities including 17 CRCC who are the Cluster Resource Coordinators. There are more than 10 supporting staff for each BEO.

The DI schools were replaced by the BEOs to provide closer supervision on the education in about 1536 primary schools in the district as smaller, more manageable units. The aim is to mainly improve the quality of education in the government schools. But how would the quality improve without the engagement of the households in the community? Rayagada is a tribal district and the population is majorly the Kondhs and the Sauras who speak Odia, Kui and Saura. What is the common language of teaching in the schools? Are the teachers trained enough to teach the students in their languages or even in an Odia comprehensible to the local children who speak a different dialect?

The plight of the schools in the district is to be seen to be believed. Only providing infrastructure, building schools, increasing access to schooling and enrolment rates is not enough for primary education. The dropout rates and low levels of learning remain challenges. Primary school enrolment in the district has been a success story, largely due to the SSA (Sarva Shiksha Abhiyan) and drives to increase enrolment even in remote blocks. But Rayagada doesn't have a primary school (class I-V) within one-kilometre walking distance. The teachers' capacity needs constant upgradation, and this has not happened regularly. Less than 700 teachers have been trained in the last couple of years with advanced content and methodology - both subject wise and class wise. But those are for higher classes. What about the primary school teachers? Who is thinking about them?

Rayagada is the woodland of Odisha's economic growth and is the mineral capital (possesses rare and coveted reserves of bauxite, manganese which is now a critical element scarce in world market and many other minerals) and yet is an Aspirational district, per Niti Ayog. It is the treasury below the soil and its children are not completing even school, forget about graduation. The CSR programs of global investments in the district have rendered nothing more than lip service to the quality of life of the people, from whom they are building their multinational conglomerates. The civil society organisations in the district are happy with the projects they get from the Metal and Mineral companies and they are far away from the communities. The local leadership is more interested in doing ancillary businesses with the industries rather than seeking more for their people. It's always more about themselves than the hapless, helpless, mute tribals. Everything happens in their name, but they are nowhere in picture.

The richest district of the state would rank among the top districts of the country for out-of-school children of primary school age, with about 12 in hundred not completing school. In many ways the schools are not equipped to handle the children – there is a teacher shortage in more than 400 primary schools, only about 60 percent of schools have functional girls' toilets and 70 percent have access to drinking water. Additionally, the quality of learning is a major issue and the children are not achieving class-appropriate learning levels.

Improving learning will require attention to details like increasing teacher accountability. Teacher attendance is appallingly low in the primary schools and raising the amount of time teachers spend on-task and increasing their responsibility for student learning also needs improvement. Teachers should not be put to 'other works. The 'other work' includes everything else other than teaching – like file work, assisting higher officials during visits, mobilising villagers for public programs and schemes. The DEO requires to conduct better assessments at each grade level and more efficient monitoring and support systems. This assessment should be regularly evaluated by the Collector. Overall, the public primary school system in Rayagada needs a better general management system, which can be done with the active leadership of the Collector. I have always maintained that the future of Odisha and India rests on the shoulders of the Collector. The civil society & the political leadership have failed the tribals.

Why can't the local industry and the civil society help the Collector and the DEO in the following:

· Build capacity and upgrade teacher education both in terms of curriculum and pedagogy, which is much needed in the local teacher education institutions like the District Education. They can initiate collaborations to facilitate technology, collaborative research projects, teacher exchanges, and subsidized online courses for teachers etc.

· Make schools better and interesting places for the children to go, instead of renovating anganwadi centres and other structures to make them look swanky. The children should not go to schools only for the midday meals. They should find school attractive.

· Use smart technology to provide high-quality, smart learning opportunities to marginalized students. Technology has a lot of potential to improve education but how it can be implemented most effectively and most cost-effectively, still remains a question. Technology comes later, only after the basic foundations are laid to make the school a place-to-go for the children. Technology should be used as a tool : as a means to an end and not an end in itself. It can be used in content creation, teacher training and classroom learning. With the help of Mo School program alumni, philanthropists and incubators can be roped in to help identify and scale best practices. A more officially driven effort is required to evaluate digital content and even more importantly to develop cost effective methods of making these available to teachers and students in Rayagada where apparently resources are scarce.

· Engage the community: deploy the village volunteers/ the BRC/the CRCC in house-to-house mobilisation for retention. The parents need to be sensitised. When they are not sensitised how do we expect the children to realise the value of completing education/schooling?

Primary education is the first and the most important foundation for a worthy life and we are neglecting that with utter arrogance.

Is it not foolish? Is it not suicidal?

Trillions of economies can happen only if we take care of our basics – complete primary education in Rayagada district is the building block.

■

India's freedom movement against NPOs (Non-performing officers)

Freeing the country from non-performing officers would free the country from the shackles binding its quantum leap in quality of life and GDP. Growth is directly proportional to the functioning, efficiency, and the behaviour of the bureaucracy. That is why the purported elitism of bureaucracy. But amoral officers take the high hat for granted and are amnesic to the fact that they owe their subsistence to the taxpayer. They are civil servants who have been selected after stringent screening, but have gone awry and off kilter, down the line. Non-performance of bright people entrusted with earth changing powers is one of the most heinous, white collar crimes. If their high capacities are not benefitting the state, then they become liabilities. I believe that the development of India, as we see today is majorly due to the skilful implementation of the schemes and policies by our bureaucracy. Because over the years our civil society and polity have been pathetically, dimming and distancing from social issues. The success in the outreach of our governance, so far, owes a lot to our bureaucracy. Though much more is desired, bureaucracy has been galvanising our policies and our development. But a few rotten apples destroy the entire pack of apples. A cabal of NPOs eat into our establishment, leaving behind an aftermath of distrust and malignment, to be encountered by the bright officers. It is time good energy drives bad energy out.

Full marks to the bold steps by the government of India and pioneering state governments to remind the officers 'perform or perish' - about their joining oaths and the expected 'civility in and of their services'. Government of India and these state governments have braved the nexus of NPOs and set off India's most wanted freedom movement of the present times – our liberation from the clutch of inept officers.

This freedom movement will guarantee us at least 40% all-round better performance in all human development indices. Our ambition of a $5 trillion economy would stagger sluggishly if the NPOs continue unabated. I have always maintained that the growth trajectory of the country rests a lot on the shoulders of the District Collectors. But NPOs create roadblocks for them. Atmanirbhar Bharat, NEP are the two pathbreaking initiatives but when it comes to implementation on the ground, it is imperative that the brakes of the NPOs be removed. Otherwise we would be going in rounds – 'making files go in circles' is the expertise of NPOs and that is the single most potent killer of our country's progress. The recent frustrations vented by our hard-working Union Ministers, State governments is palpable. They have come out openly and are committed to purge the system. The freedom movement, which ought to have snowballed with the civil society's' activism, has been flagged off by the governments. Whatever is left of our much touted "activism", invariably espouses "no-causes" but never the core issues hampering our growth. Thankfully, the well-meaning governments with temerity and strong political will are taking up the role of raising civic consciousness and responsible citizenry. Introduction of OSWAS (Odisha Secretariat Workflow Automation System) for example in Odisha has resulted in marked improvement in the decision-making system. For states like MP, Rajasthan, Odisha and some banks like the CBI have not dithered from taking steps to take strict action against non-performing employees and encouraging the many efficient ones. NPOs don't relate only to government employees. Bureaucracy is omnipresent. But government bureaucracy, additionally, is omnipotent. Like late comers to a meeting make punctual participants suffer by forcing them to wait, the POs should not suffer at the hands of the NPOs. Rather POs should drive NPOs out.

The civil society should provide complete support to the governments aiming to weed out sponges from the bureaucracy. The NPOs are more corrupt than anyone because they enjoy at the cost of the daily strugglers and common citizens of this country, with impunity. They are the vortex of inequity in our society. This inequity is our greatest developmental challenge today. The GDP suffers because of the wilful anti-development work and stand of the NPOs. NPOs do not work, because they are convinced that they enjoy a status which is imperious and unassailable. They negatively impact the system with this contagious arrogance. The NPOs need to be treated as anti-national elements. They are majorly responsible for the degradation of our productivity and the futility of our repeated attempts to rise. They damage our social fabric too.

The NPOs or the anti-nationals should be penalised

and made to retire compulsorily. This has been mooted by the Government of India and state governments like Odisha, UP, MP, Rajasthan and is full heartedly welcome. No matter how senior or significant an officer is – s/he should be afraid of losing the job if there is no performance. They should leave way for many brilliant young Indians waiting for a chance.

All of us realise the bonding of the NPO caucus and their clandestine war against such moves to clean up the bureaucracy. They would try their best to derail the movement, the same way vassals from our communities killed us much more times than the colonial rulers. Our government needs our help in extricating the NPO scourge from the nation's development. Garbage should be removed before they become carcinogenic.

I hope that the civil society supports the governments in this endeavour by judicious reporting of inefficiencies, evidence collation against wrongdoings and legitimate reporting at the right places and by adhering to the rule of law in this gargantuan task of Swach Bharat in a different avatar. A national uprising is necessary to deal with the NPO mafia.

However, responsibility lies with me.

A McKinsey report spells out that, " India is at a decisive point in its journey toward prosperity. The economic crisis sparked by COVID-19 could spur reforms that return the economy to a high-growth track and create gainful jobs for 90 million workers to 2030; letting go of this opportunity could risk a decade of economic stagnation. It aims to raise productivity and incomes for workers, small and midsize firms, and large businesses, keeping India in the ranks of the world's outperforming emerging economies."

NPOs, if allowed to thrive would mean that we all belong to the same ilk and would sully our national character. Our individual socio-economic growth and our future sustenance is heavily dependent on the kind of bureaucracy we chose to live with. The NPOs should not be emboldened by our inaction and inertness.

With unprecedented reforms in view, the governments have opened actionable fronts. The responsibility lies with us to take charge, in the interest of the nation. This is nothing short of a freedom movement to liberate all of us from the damaging atrocities of sadistic inefficiencies, the NPOs. We, the civil society with the governments' help, either cut the Gordian knot or perish under the tyranny of nonperforming Frankensteins.

Get rid of the locust or get gobbled.

God & Climate Emergency

FANI, the powerful cyclone has hit Odisha and has left a trail of destruction which has ravaged lives, destroyed families and livelihoods. Odisha region has experienced the landfall of at least four major cyclones in the last two decades which have indurated the people. Super cyclone of 1999, Phailin of 2013, Hud Hud of 2014, Titli of 2018, the blizzard of disasters, has spelt unimaginable disaster for the state and the country. But the strength to face the onslaught and recover in life, time and again has its roots in the complete faith in Lord Jagannath (Lord of the Cosmos). The literal translation of the word Jagannath means "Lord of the Universe", as it consists of the sub-words "Jagat" and "Nath". The word nath denotes "Lord" while the word "jagat" or jagan means the "universe". The Lord has been described in thousand names, Jagannath Sahasranama (in a dialogue between Yudhishtra and Bheeshma) which has a mention in the Brahma Purana (which is one of the eighteen major Puranas believed to be written by Veda Vyas and is considered the first Maha-Purana and is called the Adi Purana).

The deep entrenched belief in Odisha is that He is

the patriarch of every Odia household and is the Sole protector of every life.

The Purusha Sukta of the Rig Veda (10.7.90.1-16) spells out the supremacy of the Supreme, which is the only absolute, transcending the transcendental.

The Purusha (the Supreme Being) has a thousand heads, a thousand eyes and a thousand feet. He has enveloped this world from all sides and has transcended it.

Thus, He only exists forever, the Purushottam.

FANI had its landfall this month in Puri. The mere mortals that we are, we can't readily accept that the Lord's abode can be hit by a cyclone which has also hit us. He has to be invincible, above disasters and destruction. The previous calamities like the super cyclone or the Hud Hud had not 'reached' the temple, like it did in FANI. FANI has damaged parts of the temple. This direct storming inside the precincts of the temple has shaken the psyche of very Odia, expressed or not. As if the absolute faith in the Supreme has been assaulted. This has morally weakened every Odia more than the material loss. In spite of poverty, natural calamities, socio-economic disadvantages, Odisha has been described as the land of civility and rare comity. The civility has been a subtle manifestation of strength which comes from an absolute faith in Lord Jagannath. Has this been dented? If yes, then what could be more devastating than a fractured faith and the seeding of doubt?

I have spoken to people in the villages and urban areas and the helplessness is palpable. They don't know where to appeal. The supreme pulpit for them has been vandalised. Their faith shaken. This weakening of faith is much more damaging than material loss. Because material poverty of people was always antidoted by the anchor of trust in the Supreme.

Is this faith a subtle form of abdication from one's responsibilities? On one hand we are wedded to our faith and on the other we ravage the ecology unregretfully and invite climate change. Do we, the people, not falter in our responsibilities, which if discharged prudently would help the Supreme keep his kingdom beautiful, protected and preserved? Are we not deliberately falling prey to our chicanery for short time gains and go against the law of nature?

If we expect the Lord Jagannath to protect us and Himself, then it should be obvious for the Lord to expect discipline and morality in the people in turn. But people are watching the atrocious behaviour of the priests meted out to the pilgrims. Many irregularities or at least the publicity of the alleged wrongdoings have created irreparable cracks in the unflinching faith in the Lord.

Many I spoke to are also of the thought that the Lord, irate with the Kali Yug and the corrupt ways of the people and their world, want to teach them a lesson and make them go through hardships to realise the pristine greatness of the Universe. This sounds apocryphal but somewhere simple and easy to accept. As a story or a theory, it sounds reasonable. It is the Lord's creation and we have no right to tamper with it. We have scant respect for nature and ecology and hence have brought misery upon ourselves. Why is divinity eroding? Rituals are increasing but divinity is depleting. When a catastrophe knocks at the door, we tend to lose faith and blame the misery on the Lord or His 'apathy'.

Adi Shankaracharya writes like this in Jagannath Astakam:
na vai yâche râjyaA na cha kanaka-mâGikya-vibhavaA
na yâce 'haA ramyâA sakala jana-kâmyâA vara-vadhûm
sadâ kâle kâle pramatha-patinâ gîta-charito
jagannâtha% swâmî nayana-patha-gâmî bhavatu me (7)

I do not pray for a kingdom, nor for gold, rubies, and wealth. I do not ask for an excellent and beautiful wife as desired by all men. I simply pray that Jagannatha Swami, whose glories are always sung by Lord Siva, be the constant object of my vision.

The Supreme Lord (Purushottama Jagannath) and the Virat Purusha are the one and the same. Virat purusha, as explained by Badrayana in Brahma Sutras is the Brahman or the Avângmanasogocharam, meaning that which is incapable of being grasped by word and mind. Purushottam lies beyond the region of space, time and causation and is inconceivable by the human mind. He transcends the vyakta and the avyakta, as the experience of Markandeya Rishi (sage) is explained in Bhagavata Purana (12.9.15-34). The sage was swamped by a great deluge and was rescued after he saw Krishna as a glowing baby on a banyan tree. This banyan tree which symbolises the beginning of the universe after the great deluge (read calamity) lies inside Puri Jagannath temple and has been damaged by FANI. From the deluge to FANI, is this a complete cycle? Or are we reading too much into this because we are scared and want to clutch the last straw. The banyan tree, which is Kalpa bata, the wish fulfilling tree, is situated at the centre (Navisthala or the navel) of Sankhakhetra, Puri (conch shaped region called Puri). It is said that Jagannath Das, the author of Odia Bhagabata regarded it as the most Sacred place inside the temple premises. It is believed that Sri Chaitanya and Jagannath Das had met near Bata Ganesh and Sri Chaitanya was so impacted by the 'Bhagabata' that he embraced Jagannath Das and started addressing him by the title 'Atibadi'. The Buddhists who considered Lord Jagannath as an incarnation of Buddha compared 'Kalpabata' with Mahaboddhidruma. The tree is the embodiment of Nature, the abode of the Supreme, the Genesis.

As FANI gathered storm, the first casualty was the fluttering flag, Neelachakra Bana at the mast of the temple. It was blown away, as reported by some people who saw this to their horror and that spelt 'doom' for the believers. It was the beginning of the devastation and people panicked. Such is the 'attachment' to the Lord that the flag symbolises the 'holding of the fort' and the sovereignty of the Lord and His embrace. Without the flag, people felt the loss of the Lord's endowment. Did He choose to abandon His mortals?

The Utkala khanda of Skanda purana mentions that the Lord of the Universe, Jagannath, is the origin and the assimilation of all the 10 avataras.

ato dasavataranam darsanadyai tu yat phalam tat phalam labhate martyo drstva sri-purusottamam

"One darshan of Sri Purushottama (Lord Jagannath) is like the contemplation all the ten avataras".

Was FANI, playing destruction in the middle of Sankha kshetra or the conch region, a reminder to the mortals about the importance of balance in life? To drive reason to our minds that moderation is the answer to the wild, boundless and anti-natural ambition in life, marauding nature and its gifts. Maybe yes. This quest for answer in layers of mystery is the quest for truth, for which we have less time these days. Our journeys are gradually getting more aimless, wanton and utterly selfish. We are going away from nature, which is essentially the reason of our existence.

Was FANI a lesson, a natural cycle whose time had come, a reminder, nature's rebound action or a tight slap to correct our delinquencies? We don't know but unless we know, the purpose, if there was any at all, would be lost.

Amidst the quandary between believers and non-believers lies the fact that it's a repeat call to action. In my perspective, nature and super nature are the same set of cosmic templates and it is quintessential that we respect nature. Climate change is not a jargon or a developmental theme anymore. It is here and now.

Malika, a prophecy by saint Achyutananda Das seems to suggest that one day the deities will abandon their abode as Puri will be submerged by the sea due to global warming and subsequent rise in water level. This gains more currency among the believers because it is construed that his prediction in Malika about the 1866 great famine, 1999 super cyclone, currently soaring heat waves due to global warming and other major catastrophes in the country have come true.

This is no doomsday prophecy nor is this an apology or an alibi. It is the truth that unless we treat nature, which we have not created but are enjoying, with ultimate reverence, even Lord of the Cosmos will suffer. He would suffer because he is Bhakta's Bhagwan or the believer's Lord. Lord Jagannath is absolutely devotee-centric. He can't desert the devotee. For any mortal who serves Him with complete faith, both in prosperity and adversity, He always reciprocates. He is blindly in love with His faithful devotees.

sattvânurûpâ sarvasya úraddhâ bhavati bhârata
œraddhmayoyam puruso yo yacchraddhah sa eva sah

"O descendent of Bharata, faith manifests in everyone (or everywhere) according to sattva. A person is made up of faith only. He is surely what his faith is."

(Bhagavad Gita: Chapter 17 Sloka 03)

The Supreme is here with us.

Naaham teesthaami vaikunthe, yoginaam hridaye na cha
Madbhaktaa yatra dhyaayanti tatra teesthaami naarada

Neither have I stayed in the heaven nor even in the heart of saints. I reside in that place where my devotees pray / worship

Let's pray to nature and rebuild the faith.

Rest assured.

■

Art & Life in Odisha

Art is the proper task of life, said Nietzsche and Bertolt Brecht thinks that "if art reflects life, it does so with special mirrors". Maybe yes but both the thoughts are conjoint. Art is certainly a proper task and reflects life in diverse paradigms without deviating from the influence of centrality, which is life itself. The self-conscious aim of life is to find expression, and art offers it beautiful forms through which life gets interlaced in a 'mirror-continuum'. We are all the sum of the parts of our history, present and future and as guardians of the age, we reflect the zeitgeist and spirit of the times and enkindle the culture. Art is the lighthouse of times in transition. Odisha in its journey through different rulers, cultural forms and influences has taken recourse in its art, its alter ego, Art. The intimacy is palpable.

The sublime, cultured way of life of Odisha is adequately manifested by widespread and eclectic art forms across the state. This article attempts to cite a few examples of the intertwining of art and life in Odisha, in select settings, art forms and geographies.

Khiching town in Mayurbhanj district basks in antediluvian romance of art and heritage which flaunts the culture of seamless secularism (multiple faiths like Buddhism, Jainism & Brahmanism) were practiced and the antiquities unearthed from the sites around the Kichakeswari temple and other adjoining places reveal immaculate art work. In various forms, from stone carving to colour painting and sketches, the craftsmanship of ancient Khiching artisans and their architectural finesse is alive at Maa Kichakeswari temple, Kuteitundi temple, Chandrasekhar temple, forts and places at Kichakgarh and Biratgarh. Life in Odisha has been culturally vibrant and progressive. Baripada Museum was set up in 1903 and Khiching Museum in 1922 and these two museums pioneered archaeological documentation in Odisha, unknown then, under the British rule in Odisha.

Music is adjudged as one of the most impactful among 64 types of arts. Jayadeva's Gita Govind celebrated the mortal-creator unity in an atmosphere of musical creativity, romance and synergy with the daily routines of soulful piety. The love between Radha and Krishna, that he created, was an allegory for spirituality – a theme which was later developed Sri Chaitanya. The use of various *rasas*, the usage of the concept of "Ashtanayika" to describe the full range of emotions, with eight different moods of a heroine have majorly influenced the development of classical Indian dance forms. In Odisha, the performance of the *Gita Govinda* as a drama is central to Odissi, the classical dance form that originated from the temples of Odisha and portrayed the Odisha life and culture.

The unflinching belief in "befriending" the Supreme continues to pervade Odisha belief system. Lord Jagannath, the Supreme deity of Odisha is the "bhaktara bhagwan" or the "Lord of the devotee". He is the friend, philosopher and guide of every Odisha household and embodies love as the only means of reaching Him. The Odia belief is one of intense devotion, passion; poetry, song and dance. Millions in Rath Yatra worldwide, celebrate life in riots of colours, different dances and music in the forms of bhajans and Kirtans. The carnival is a roadshow of art & culture, unparallel in the world, in sheer scale diversity and intensity. Prof Knut A. Jacobsen of University of Bergen observes that the *Rathayatra* as an event has a major community heritage, social sharing and cultural significance for the society at large. Jagannath is the core of Odishan way of life. Motifs of *jhooti (traditional odia art in white colour made from rice paste and created using fingers on the wall and floor surfaces)* across the state bear Jagannath-centric symbols and patterns. These jhootis are now considered hip designs used in saree and other garment prints.

Jhooti design

Tribal dances like dhap, banabadi, ghumura, chutkichuta, rasarkali, bajasaal and singari are an integral of festivities connected with different activities in the life of tribals - sowing, harvesting and consumption of first fruits, shifting cultivations, slash and burn method of soil treatment. The tribals worship nature and hence the paintings, dances and music are concomitant to the life of tribals – free spirited, progressive, moderately ritualistic and aligned to the flow of life and nature. The Santhals for example have a special spring festival of rejoicing with sprinkling of water, special songs and dances. The women-centric figures and sketches in the Bonda paintings in Malkangiri district reflect the matriarchal order in the community. Women are empowered and are the principal decision makers in a family and the community. The style of music and the sartorial preferences among the Juang, Bhuyan, Kondh, Saura, Gadaba, Jharia, Didayee, Koya and Bonda, tribes spread across Ganjam Malkangiri, Koraput, Rayagada, Kalahandi, Sundargarh, Boudh and Phulbani districts of Odisha primarily display agriculture as the central theme and exhibit allied community life centering around cultivation (includes sub themes like first-fruit eating, live-stock and crop welfare), livelihoods community well-being and group solidarity. Music and dance have traditionally played an important role in Odishan culture, specifically the tribals, who constitute more than twenty percent of the state population. Ancient tribal culture encompassed music into their everyday lives. Dance, story-telling and religious practices are all grounded on the music of the culture. In many ways, the tribal music and art is a utilitarian function used in vital aspects of life such as, a child's naming ceremony, initiation rights, agricultural activities, national ceremonies, religious ceremonies and ceremonies for the dead.

  Tribal paintings are original in idea and execution and the santhal and saura tribes accord them the dignity not found commonly. These paintings express the life of the tribes in which offerings made to the nature/forest gods, ancestors and spirits are much valued. The *Saura* tribes draw pictographs on the inner and outer walls of their mud dwellings called 'Ittlans' and the accent is on nature, the scenic outdoors and on the cycle of ploughing, sowing & harvesting. Above all the daily life and its inherent beauty. Nature is shackle free and so are the people of nature who are bohemian and know the art of appreciating nature and its limitless mystery.

Saura painting

The first Oriya Magazine of *Bodha Dayini* published from Balasore in 1861 not only promoted Odia literature by providing a consistent platform but ventilated social thoughts on governance, through its well-researched writings. The first Oriya newspaper, The Utkal Deepika in 1866 encouraged modern and creative literature and mirrored life in those times. Radhanath Ray's long verses like Chandrabhaga, Nandikeshwari, Usha, Mahajatra, Darbar and Chilika essayed the beauty and grind of life, under the western influence. Fakir Mohan Senapati, the doyen of modern Odia fiction, revolutionised Odia literature through a unique style combining realism, conciseness and portrayals closer to life and yet enigmatic. *Chha Maana Atha Guntha* cried about peasant exploitation much before the Russian October revolution turned into an 'ism'.

Sambalpuri sarees with designs based on Chitra Kabya Bandhodaya authored by legendary Odia poet Kabi Samrat Upendra Bhanja depict the romance of life in Odisha. And contemporary textile designs are exhibiting the Devadasi/Mahari dance form of Odisha (social trends), celebrating art which reflects the divinity and grace of Odisha life.

Art is infinite and multifarious. While we, oscillate between the Aristotelian mimesis, (that art imitates life) or the Oscar Wilde anti-mimesis (that life imitates art), I would reiterate that Art & Life have been and continue to be the inseparables in Odisha. In every form, though in this article I have mentioned only a few of them, art unites lives and expresses life in myriad lens - from flirtation with imagery of the human body and self-portraiture and regular life, to expressing something comparatively intangible, a recurring psychological motif such as a state of mind, piety, a mood or a memory.

Life itself is an art. A true work of art is but a shadow of the divine perfection. Indeed, even those who regard art as an ideal and artists as idealists agree that art is a faithful mirror of the life and civilization of a period.

Art and life go together in Odisha and hence the soft power of Odisha.

■

Meeting Mr Mehta

I am not writing this because he was well connected but because I felt connected to him. A memorable one even if we had a brief meeting more than a decade and half ago in NY. We were at a dinner hosted by an American tech entrepreneur interested in social investments across the globe, specifically India. It was a hip socialite, (read HNWI) evening at a Manhattan high rise, surrounded by number rattling economists, their rather cold partners and a few high octane social changemakers trying to combat numbers with the emotions of life changing stories, mostly from developing geographies of south Asia. Frankly it was quite another rigmarole for me.

Enters Mr Mehta and all eyes towards him. He was introduced then as one of the best-known Asian's in the elite circles of the globe. Of course, his Knopf entity and the other accreditations followed. But for me he stood out clearly as the "palpably most knowledgeable person" in the motley gathering of about 50. He shone brilliance. When in a sub-subgroup we were together in a corner, I had a feeling that I knew him since long. Affable and yet distant,

I found him very real. So, rooted that when we discussed about Bollywood, poverty in South Asia, Nicaragua rebels, commercialisation of sports, he was unstoppable, though quiet. Not did I attempt to. I was never from the fourth estate and never knew him then as the high priest of global publishing, but that beautiful NY evening gave me a super eclectic acquaintance. I wasn't sure whether we would meet again, but I was sure that 'this tete-a-tete' was for keeps for life. A brilliant mind, he was absolutely non-judgemental and perhaps that is why he was one of the world's most successful publishers. He could see stars when others lost out in 'reading the pulse'.

In the dinner meet he was the celebrity. He spoke very little but spoke intense. Smartly turned out he was always in the 'centre' of the discussion revolving around tech enterprises, investment banking, social investment, and new age philanthropists. If he was the senior most in age, he was the erudite most in his viewpoints. Admirably contemporary, genuinely cosmopolitan and magnet of the dinner party, Mr Mehta exuded a rare "cultured erudition".

The next day my family described more about him and his connections with Odisha. My respect for him goes up many notches because in our conversation we spoke about Odisha, the economy and the social equity but never, even as a passing remark he mentioned anything about his family in Odisha, which could be even remotely construed as 'flaunting".

He was the first family of world publishing and back home his was the first family of Odisha – but for the evolved Mr Mehta, he was what he was.

Mr Mehta supported our social initiative, the dinner party was a great meeting of great minds, life moved on, but indelible was his presence and our skull session. I had met him in Delhi once, after NY and this time we discussed about books, authors and the changing trends.

There is something incredibly nostalgic and significant about meeting Mr Sonny Mehta.

He was luminous and he was the best - considered "the best published" in the world.

Sometimes, rarely, you meet someone like Mr Mehta. RIP

■

Nostalgia - Smruti tume...

You are the nostalgia,
Of,
the unseen touch of the spring
the monsoon night,
the ash laden smouldering fire
You are the nostalgia
Of,
the danseuse encircled temple foyer,
the melancholic moon between the
twigs of the Casuarina woodlands,
You are the nostalgia
Of
the charcoal scribbled name
in the motel,
the hamlet of my last love.
You are the nostalgia
Of,
the faded *alata* on
the beach rock,
You are the nostalgia
Of,
the terrible eventide

on a widow's temple,
You are the nostalgia
Of,
A paper boat,
On an irreversible river
You are my nostalgia,
Oh
So beloved.

(English adaptation of the brilliant Odia song Smruti tumey.. by the legendary Akshaya Mohanty. The lyrics and composition of the song is by the versatile genius Akshaya Mohanty)

—
Smruti tume...
srabana rati
adekha chaiti chuaann.
Smruti tume paaunsa tala ra niaa
Smruti tume .
nartaki ghera mandira mukhasala...
Smruti tume... jhaaun bana fanke .karuna chandra kala
Smruti tume panthasala re angaare lekha naa
Smurti tume bigata priya ra gaann...

Smruti tume tutha pathara re
fika alata ra daga
Smruti tume bidhaba lalate
daruna astaranga
Smruti tume aphera nadi re
kagaja tiari naa
Smruti tume mora ati priyatama ahaaaaa

Strangely there is no airport at Brahmapur, Odisha

Brahmapur was the epicentre of Odia sub nationalism and the movement for Odisha state formation gained momentum from the Ganjam alma mater of freedom struggle. The 'silk city' known worldwide for silk related enterprise is today the commercial hub closest to the SEZ at Gopalpur – the Gopalpur Industrial park. It is growing at scorching pace, aiming to be India's biggest multi-product Special Economic Zone and located strategically at Gopalpur- at-sea. Gopalpur, once the favourite resort of Britishers, was also a commercially successful Port and continues to be so. The contribution of Gopalpur port to the GDP of India would be significant and in the coming years when we are aspiring for a $ 5 trillion economy, it would provide the infrastructural support and gateway by providing access to a cargo variety covering minerals, steel, aluminium, cement, illuminate coal, CP Coke, steel products, industrial salt, granite blocks, BF slag & fertilizers. By 2030 Gopalpur port is projected to be one of the major ports of India. The government is gearing up to set up a

Bulk Drug Park within the Tata Steel Special Economic Zone (SEZ) at Gopalpur. The proposed project is part of the state government's aim of creating employment opportunities through industrialization in the non-mineral sector. The location of the proposed drug park spot is well connected with port and railway. The land is well connected with NH-16 which is considered as the spine for the proposed Odisha Economic Corridor.

Gopalpur has the unique distinction of being one of the most natural beaches of India, attracting foreigners and domestic tourists. Besides being an international port for the seafarers of ancient Kalinga, it served as an important military port during the World War –I, from where soldiers sailed to Burma. Ganjam's connection with Burma has always been strong and deep rooted. It was in Gopalpur where Odisha's first luxury hotel and the country's first-of-its-kind beach resort was built. The Palm Beach Resort was built in 1914 by Signor Maglioni and was later acquired by the Oberoi group of hotels in 1948. This is believed to be the iconic group's first property in hospitality business, even predating Shimla business.

Brahmapur, the port city is one of the oldest cities of India, known for its rich legacy in women art, weaving and enterprise. Since Brahmapur continues to be commercial junction of south Odisha, the market caters to more than half of the state. It houses major educational institutes, medical colleges, hospitals.

It is a travesty that Brahmapur, in spite of emerging as the nucleus of heritage, commerce and national growth, does not have an airport till date.

Brahmapur has one of the oldest airstrips of India, at Rangeilunda which can be expanded to a full-capacity airport. Many people from various ministries have inspected the site but what is lacking is concrete action on the ground.

Students, faculties, corporates visit Brahmapur frequently due to the presence of national institutes like the Army AD college, NIST, IISER, two large Universities, one prominent Medical College of eastern India, and eight engineering colleges. The nearest airport is 200 kms (Bhubaneswar and Vishakpatnam) away and this affects the business and careers, negatively. One of the revered Buddhist sites of Asia at Jeerango, and the Ashokan Rock edict at Jaugada are international tourist sites. But without an airport it is a logistics nightmare for international tourists to come to the sites.

One major shock for the people of Ganjam was the non-selection of Brahmapur as a IIM site. Starting from its days in the Madras Presidency, to its contribution to national freedom struggle to the present-day emergence as a major business district in the national economic corridor, Brahmapur and the larger district of Ganjam deserve better treatment. The contiguous geographies of southern Odisha and northern Andhra is cobbled together by Ganjam district. It would not be an exaggeration to assert that the Odia diaspora, across the world, cutting across skill levels (white collar or blue collar) would count the highest from Ganjam. The remittances to Ganjam is one of the highest in the state and the entire eastern region.

But there is no facility for a smooth homecoming for our diaspora. Air travel to Odisha/AP (Bhubaneswar/Vizag) and then road or rail travel to Ganjam is a nightmare. There is enough demand and economic preparedness in prospective customers to make airlines feasible, if they ply from Delhi or Mumbai to Brahmapur.

The famed hard-working people of Ganjam district

need expanding their businesses. The silk saree business is in a slump, the SEZ needs more investments, the modern port wants aggressive partnerships, the tourism industry is hungry for longer stay durations of international travellers and the son of the soil, the non resident Odia is longing to visit home and invest in his or her people and resources.

The single most important factor that can catapult the State of Odisha to be one of the major contributors to national growth is air linkage to Brahmapur. The impact of this infrastructural support will not only benefit Odisha but AP too. In these times, one cannot and should not confine socio economic development to a geography. It is seamless.

The citizens of Ganjam would be glad to participate in any kind of feasibility study or DPR to get the airport up and running at Brahmapur, as soon as possible. It will change the face of development in our lifetimes.

Odisha preparing for high speed growth – New RI Cirlces

After a long time, since the major Panchayati Raj reforms were done in the 90s, the plan to create 450 new revenue circles came as bold governance steps to prepare the state for mega growth plans. By 2030, I foresee Odisha to contribute much over 6% to the national GDP. If we can manage the investments, skill our youth to get absorbed in Odisha, particularly in the minerals, SME and services sector, there is nothing that can stop the state to assert itself by sheer contribution to India's growth story. Odisha holds the key to the national vision of $5 trillion economy. Big ticket investments are flowing in and many are in the pipeline. Investment needs a basic core or a foundation to help it achieve triple bottom line. Odisha should exhort the investing corporates to work sustainably in the state. The three bottom lines or the three P's: people, planet, and profit have to be assured. With the auction of mines, growth in manufacturing, specifically in SME sector, implementation of the Kalia scheme to cover more than 16% of the population we need efficiency in governance.

The PRI (Panchayati Raj Institutions), Zilla Parishads, Panchayats are still underutilised.

Odisha is a gifted land in the world because it has a mix of all – the natives who are rich with mineral resources, the unique art and crafts of skilled people with unbelievable piety and unparallel soft skills and invaluable land mass to foster rapid industrial growth (480 kms coast, large numbers of water bodies, reasonably higher ground water table, over 310 sunny days yearly, increasing forest cover) and trouble free labour force. The long coastline contains Asia's second largest eco-system of mangroves and some of the world's richest biodiversity. We are aiming at making Bhubaneswar the skill capital of India and ideally Odia youths should be employed there. But industrialisation has to be rapid. The perennial question – can we or should we abandon the globally unique and superabundant flora and fauna and run the rat race towards destruction, pollution and contamination. I would not have been worried about industrialisation if we knew how to tackle development along with clean environment, if we knew how to enforce ecological discipline among the companies playing with natural and mineral resources, if we knew how to respect the PVTGs, if we knew how to handle exploitation of land, labour and faith. Because Odisha should not, at any cost lose its pristine wealth, its blessed existence and the benediction. From Puri, the seat of Odia spirituality to Rayagada the woodland of Odia economic growth, tribality is the profound underline. It's all about tribals, from the Lord to the Mining, but they are the most deprived, utterly neglected and severely cornered.

Odisha is the treasure house. No other state in India has comparable wealth - large reserves of bauxite (65%), chinaclay, chromite (98.3%), coal (27%), dolomite (20.7%), fireclay, graphite (76.67%), gemstones, iron ore (26%), limestone, manganese ore (31.7%), mineral sand, nickel ore (95.1%), pyrophyllite, diamond and quartz. The stack of other minerals includes copper ore, lead ore, titanium bearing magnetite, talc/ soap stone and high magnesia igneous rocks. Odisha possesses almost all of India's chromite, graphite, nickel, bauxite, high quality coal iron ore, beach sand. Yet the contribution of Odisha to national GDP is unconvincingly low.

For investments to fructify in the state we need to have a fast track system of handling land settlement efficiently and timely. The government schemes are not reaching people adequately due to eligibility bottlenecks and clearances at the last mile. If the social security is taken care of, then it is expected that the investments would not result in wanton commercial growth at the cost of the happiness and all-round growth of the people.

So far the role of the civil society has been queasy and limited. We are aware that investment-friendly policies, good governance, robust infrastructure, mineral resources and agriculture resources and access to the market can make Odisha a complete development destination. But it all starts with the opening of the lock at the community. We are talking of development of the state and do we forget that development means 'of the people, by the people and for the people'. In this discourse of development, the only word scarcely used is 'People'. Only a Gram Sabha reminds us of the rights of the people to decide about themselves. But who works towards sensitising the communities who constitute the Gram Sabha? Where are the civil society organisations, the NGOs? On one hand we have activists promoting their ISMs in the name of being pro poor and on the other hand we have CSR programs of industries engaged in tokenism in the name of development. Gram Sabha is the only key to development, bottoms up. This because Gram Sabha is where the action lies. It is the council holding the key to the development of the country. If Odisha is the gold mine and the global repository, then Gram Sabha is the door to the treasure. More so, when we are discussing rental economy. But how do we strengthen the district and the below district governance which would have a direct bearing on the wellness of the State?

The creation of new RI circles would take the total number in the state to 2729, after 450 more circles would be added. The RIs would be separate for rural and urban areas - in rural areas, one revenue circle will be created for three GPs (gram panchayats). In the municipal areas one RI (Revenue Inspector) would be placed for three municipal wards. The urban centres, include Bhubaneswar, Cuttack, Rourkela, Berhampur, Puri and Sambalpur. There can't be an absolute measurement of the contribution of this governance exercise to the state GDP but it won't be an exaggeration to conclude that we can term the investments successful if the output boosts Odisha's economy and human development index.

The scaling up of RI circles is a great and timely enabler but deployment of officers could be a challenge and so the selection and recruitment boards need to be concurrently empowered and mandated to go for large scale recruitments.

Odisha is preparing big time and if we don't get ready with strong below district governance, we might as well forget trillions in economy.

■

Ministry of Thinking

*A*fter all these years of independence we have not done much to foster thinking in our young minds. India is a land of unlimited capabilities. Now the time has come for a Ministry of Thinking to make systemic interventions in promoting thinking with a mission and vision in place – thinking with a direction. Human capital should be rescued form being only a jargon.

I have been meeting and Interacting with below 35's across India who are graduates, use internet and majority of them want to follow their friends in career choices. Less than 15 in a hundred, think and decide to pursue their calling. What about the rest? Today the average age of an Indian is 29 years and by now s/he should be peaking in imagination. But they cannot, even if they want to. Where is the thinking? Have we created a space for them to think? Public schemes, start-up drives, policies come much later. The foundation is the development of the young mind – a personal journey.

Google, Airbnb, Uber, LinkedIn, Tripadvisor, Spotify and Whatsapp and a million others provide the youngster a secured avenue to adapt his or her skills to the common mission of a large technology corporate. But before joining the technology bandwagon, where does s/he get the space to imagine? Moreover, the youngsters need to detach from technology to focus on thinking. A study in America says that more time is spent watching Netflix than with friends. Thinking appears nowhere in the list. There is death of idle brain time. The drivers these days can't drive even normal routes without google maps on their phones. A few years ago, they exercised their memories to remember complicated by-lanes of old cities like Lucknow or Cuttack. But no more. During COVID our workplace and home are the same place. There is no 'me time' or 'home time'. Your gadgets and you have to be blinking 24X7. Even sports outings are no escapes - accessorised by Apple watch & Fitbits of the world.

Where are you? Can you be with yourself?

Time has come when we, as the youngest community of the world, need to institutionalise thinking. An exclusive Ministry of Thinking should be mandated with the task of enhancing the thinking power of the country, infant onwards. This Ministry alone would have the potential of changing the face of this country, increasing its endowments, and making it the fountainhead of human development. Our Ministries – HRD, Education, Social welfare, Social Justice, Women & Child, Science & Technology, and others have not been able to work on our foundation, i.e. our imagination. They are still at the periphery, even after 7-8 decades of relentless need for new thinking. Human minds are meant for creativity, but we have kept them asphyxiated.

We ought to make thinking a part of the school, college and workplace routines. There are many clubs or youth groups in colleges but there is hardly any on 'thinking'. Our brains are otherwise overstimulated but strangely not to be with oneself and on self-thoughts. The peer pressure for youths is all about personality and the quiet introverts desperately attempt to emulate extroverts. The youths have to live with the stress of not being "true to themselves" and become physically and mentally ill. I had been 'doctored' in B school to place extroverts at higher esteem because they were 'chosen' as charismatic and self-assured. But later in life I realised that they burnt out early, suffered from lack of ingenuity and grew more and more unsuitable for changing times. Our entire work culture in the eighties and nineties was built on structuring performance around the garrulous extrovert-ism. This has damaged our individual, quiet and inventive thinking. The quietly contemplative, well-informed and mostly from vernacular medium schooling need their space under the sun to think and nurture their originality rather than being almost forced to be swept away in the flash storm of the dominant 'thoughtless and overvalued', puffed *no-thinks*.

The way forward, for our country is to create 'chapters of thinking' at the state, district and sub-districts that have open-plan bits for both the extroverts or the 'exposed few' and the quiet people. The hackathons are getting confined to only a few closed groups. Without a deliberate national plan and interventions more and more of our idle brain and thinking time would disappear. Our net innovations will decrease, our youths would stagnate.

Idle mind is required for innovations. Schools, colleges should allocate special classes for thinking. Critical thinking is fast disappearing. Today's flood of non-stop and made to customised visual entertainment impairs our critical thinking. In this entertainment we have everything already visualised for us. They are all image based and fast paced. Obviously, our tendency is to spend less time reading, thinking and exercising our imagination. Book reading should be a program sub-set, under the Ministry of Thinking. The public libraries need to be dusted, rekindled and their profiles raised. If done doggedly, libraries will become our "development labs." Reading triggers imagination. As a below 29 country, our imagination could be our biggest arsenal. We need to make thinking a national practice and agenda.

Innovations need not remain confined to only the technology domain. Non technological creativity is not given the deserving status. Do you hear of any new form of writing? Painting? Dance, accorded the hype of a breakthrough? Even if given, it is rare and exceptional. Almost none, barring films, and only after proven success in the box office or the idiot box.

Thinking is the new vaccine, a preventive that would protect our economy much better than anything else. Today those who spend more time reading, thinking, and imagining will own an increasingly large advantage over those who do not think and act original. The world as we have created so far is a process of our thinking. It cannot be changed without changing our thinking. Robert Gordon, an economics professor of repute laments that "the days of great inventions are over". Economists typically measure innovation with the total factor productivity (TFP) and sometime back he observed that "falling productivity is one of the main reasons for growth shortfall in advanced economies like the United States. It is not an end to innovation, but a decline in the usefulness of future inventions that is taking place. Moreover, the newer innovations do not seem to be benefitting all segments of society, which in turn reflects rising inequality in the advanced countries." In India, TFP growth was 3.5% in 2016, 1.6% in 2017 and 2.4% in 2018. Our vision of $5 trillion economy would require growing at 8% in real terms and supported by a 0.7% + rise in TFP. How do we achieve this without thinking?

No problem can withstand the assault of sustained thinking is what Voltaire had said famously. If English, Yoga, vernacular language use, health check ups are made compulsory in schools, so should 'thinking' – the most original, unique and basic human existential value.

The Ministry's work would be to collect individual thinking and turn them to collective human capital – the only capital which is sustainable and endlessly augmentable.

New Year 2021, New Chief Secretary

There is a change in guard and a new captain will start his new innings, though on the same pitch. 2021 will be an important year of pushing development agenda in the middle of the COVID aftermath.

The Chief secretary (CS) position is the peak of a bureaucrat's career in the state. We, the people expect the incoming CS to lead the state administration from the front, develop a youthful, futuristic ethos and reduce inefficiencies in the outreach of public schemes. The dependency on the government for welfare activities will keep increasing in Odisha and in another 5 years would be at its apogee. Because the role of civil society organisations (CSOs) is almost elegiacal. By 2025 we wouldn't expect CSOs to be involved in any social development issues. Regretfully, they would continue to be confined to the role of outsourced agencies for implementing projects. Hence all the thinking, planning and execution of public goods distribution would have to be done by the government. Involvement of the village and district youth in public work is an idea whose time has come. We have hopes of the CS taking smart strides in ushering in the incipient but warranted paradigm shift in the state development. COVID has changed our lives and will continue to do so in the next 2-3 years, during which our below 35 age population would increase by about 4%. Ganjam, Cuttack, Balasore, Khordha, Mayurbhanj districts are the high population districts which would need special attention as far as the preparedness to combat the mutant coronavirus is concerned.

The new incumbent CS would have a tenure of slightly more than twelve months and that is a good time period to bring about the following changes: (at least rev up the mechanisms)

- Make development the central narrative: As long as it helps development of the state, it doesn't really matter whether the help is coming from the centre or the state. So the proposals and the policy work in the state needs further polishing and push. E.g, in the last five years Odisha has received Rs 7744.68 Cr as CAMPA fund. The expenditure has been hardly 50%. With super-high intensity of mining in Odisha, the rate of afforestation is poor. Agreed that it is often difficult to find the non-forest land for afforestation to compensate the loss of forest. But a special task force has to be given the task to complete the first phase by next monsoons. This is high priority because we are in the middle of climate emergency.

- Help solve on-going and long-standing border disputes with all our neighbouring States: i.e. Andhra Pradesh, West Bengal, Jharkhand and Chhattisgarh. Odisha should take the lead in initiating bilateral discussions with the border states. I have been advocating for the resolution of Kotia Panchayat (Koraput) case with Andhra and there are fourteen out of Odisha's 30 districts which share borders and are in litigation with other states. There is a long history of border and water disputes which are waiting for resolutions due to historical, cartographic and geological reasons. This will have direct impact on the livelihoods & socio-economic interest of our people living in the troubled geographies. Our resources are too coveted to be frittered away in avoidable challenges.

· Make Livelihoods initiatives aggressive: More than 25 percent of the state population consist of indigenous people and over 90 percent of farmers are small and marginal land holders. They depend on agriculture and allied sectors as their primary sources of income. Let us be realistic. According to some estimates, Odisha has more than 2.5 million migrant workers, and since the 90s, there is principally "migrarian" livelihoods, with migration and agriculture as the major providers. In April 2020, data collated by CMIE showed that the unemployment rate in Odisha was 23.8%. it is not easy to expect large scale absorption of the unemployed under MGNREGS. Almost two-thirds of the migrants are back to the cities. The only way to ensure employment or gainful engagement is to create opportunities in the state. Livelihoods initiative does not mean only rural livelihoods. The women groups of the state need to be federated more and given support to start their producer organisations – both in rural and urban areas. By 2022, management of urban population would be a major challenge in Odisha. Bhubaneswar is now bursting at its seams, Berhampur is lagging much behind in city management, Rourkela is getting inundated with slums with each passing day, Sambalpur is looking for development, Cuttack needs help. Old Bhubaneswar (temple area) and Puri temple area cleaning and modernisation are global examples of community supported, cleansing of age-old decadence. But these islands of success need to be replicated across the state.

· Make Odisha communication vigorous: The ongoing advertisement blitzkrieg by Odisha Tourism is commendable. The quality and the strategic placement of the commercials in national and international media is praiseworthy. The peace and easy pace of life, the stability of the state and the soft skills of people need to be highlighted. In the coming decades, capital investments would be largely determined by the softer life-elements. The ease-of-doing factor would be largely governed by the participation of the people in the business. So, the "people factor" is the crucial smart factor to be nurtured and disseminated. In each of the big cities where we have optimal sized Odia associations (Delhi, Mumbai, Bangalore, Chennai, Pune, Goa) we should engage them in Talking about Odisha in their social, professional and economic spheres. This can be done with planned, subtle but sustainable interventions.

· Invigorate Odisha representation: Tourism, Industries, Handloom & Handicraft, Culinary need to be exported to the rest of the country and the Region. The government of Odisha outfit in Delhi should reach out to prospective investors, do high quality roadshows, organise intellectual discussions about Odisha and its potentials in ramped up frequency, intensity and visibility. Delhi is the capital of the ambitious $5 tn economy and there should be competitive states' demands and high energy sales pitch. Delhi belongs to every state of the country and we need to create our niche. When you are next in Delhi during one of your official visits, you should get prudent and progressive feedback. Similarly, at Mumbai.

Vietnam, Philippines, South Korea, Thailand, some

CIS countries are the fast emerging economies and as early as 2025 they would be strongly placed in the manufacturing, electronics sectors. For example, Vietnam's manufacturing sector has grown exponentially since 2010 because businesses have started to look elsewhere as labour costs in China increased. The ongoing US-China fracas has made China a less attractive place to manufacture, with a number of tariffs on exports. Many multinationals have started operating in Vietnam, including global technology leaders like Apple and Samsung. Odisha could make special efforts to engage in dialogues with Vietnam (also other countries) in outsourcing of manufacturing facilities. This will be a win-win proposition.

· Handling NPOs (non-performing officers): Freeing the state from non-performing officers would free all of us from the shackles binding its quantum leap in quality of life and GDP. Growth is directly proportional to the functioning, efficiency, and the behaviour of the bureaucracy. That is why the purported elitism of bureaucracy. But amoral officers take the high hat for granted and are amnesic to the fact that they owe their subsistence to the taxpayer. They are civil servants who have been selected after stringent screening, but have gone awry and off kilter, down the line. Non-performance of bright people entrusted with earth changing powers is one of the most heinous, white collar crimes. If their high capacities are not benefitting the state, then they become liabilities. I believe that the development of Odisha, as we see today is majorly due to the skilful implementation of the schemes and policies by our bureaucracy. Because over the years our civil society and polity have been pathetically, dimming and distancing from social issues. The success in the outreach of our governance, so far, owes a lot to our bureaucracy. Though much more is desired, bureaucracy has been galvanising our policies and our development. But a few rotten apples destroy the entire pack of apples. A cabal of NPOs eat into our establishment, leaving behind an aftermath of distrust and malignment, to be encountered by the bright officers. It is time good energy drives bad energy out.

Full marks to the bold steps by the government of India and pioneering state governments like ours, to remind the officers 'perform or perish' - about their joining oaths and the expected 'civility in and of their services'. Government of India and these state governments have braved the nexus of NPOs and set off India's most wanted freedom movement of the present times – our liberation from the clutch of inept officers.

This freedom movement will guarantee us at least 40% all-round better performance in all human development indices. Our ambition of a $5 trillion economy would stagger sluggishly if the NPOs continue unabated. I have always maintained that the growth trajectory of the country rests a lot on the shoulders of the District Collectors. But NPOs create roadblocks for them.

NPOs don't relate only to government employees. Bureaucracy is omnipresent. But government bureaucracy, additionally, is omnipotent. Like the punctual participants who suffer due to the late comers to a meeting who force them to wait, the POs (performing officers) should not suffer at the hands of the NPOs. Rather POs should drive NPOs out. POs should be felicitated and gloriously rewarded.

The wish list is unending. But we do hope that 2021, under CS's guidance, helps Odisha find balance on its feet, engage youngsters, and tackle natural disasters, as much as possible and even more.

A lot of hope till Feb 2022, at least.

Balakrushna Dash – the Renaissance Man of Odia music

He defied the norm that "urbanites mainly compose modern music". From a humble background, Sangeeta Sudhakara Balakrushna Dash, reached heights in Odia music in all forms – filmy & non-filmy. So confident he was of his craft that even in the big city Calcutta he was not shy or gauche. The overwhelming Bengali music and film didn't wean him away from legitimate Odissi, chanda or bhajan (devotional songs). His career (singing to begin with) took off at Calcutta but he maintained his Odia exclusivity, and never inveigled himself into the Bengali wave. The title Sangeeta Sudhakar is apt for this genius whose music was modern and yet copybook, futuristic in orchestration and yet folksy. One can smell Odisha soil in his music. The lyrics he chose were tailor made to his punch – the impeccable mix of homemade and commercial. This repertoire came to him naturally and all his contemporaries and juniors have been overawed with his range of compositions in all these decades. He was a naturally gifted prodigy with deep grounding in classical music, under the tutelage of greats like Ustad Bade Gulam Ali Khan. Sir's early initiation into music in a place like Calcutta exposed him to different styles and penchants in singing, composition and finer elements like orchestration. Till he burst into Odia music scene, there was virtually nothing much happening in orchestration. No one experimented with limited instruments and limited sequencing in films, the way he did. His music transformed film viewing. S.D.Burman and Balakrushna Dash had a similar indistinguishable knack in transforming folk tunes and traditional lyrics to catchy melody, irrespective of language or filmy demands. I have heard from my father, who had written lyrics for him, that Balakrushna Sir was a polymath in music – his grasp of the sequence of the scene and the befitting mood was unique and unparalleled. All of the twenty-two films where he has scored were musical hits. His hit rate was cent percent, reflecting the depth of his understanding of various genres.

Balakrushna Sir used folk fervour, never ever waivered Odia intensity and yet gave hit after hits – almost a run of about 15 films nonstop, back to back hits. He was the first experimenter of Odia music, the composer who brought in authentic western style to filmy music, used instruments like piano and trumpet in early 60's and at the same time engrossed himself full time in Radio – with Odissi, Drama, Bhajan, classical and even theatre. Sometimes unprepared, unrehearsed he would have a perfect single take of difficult compositions. Such was the genius that even a well-known, maverick lifestyle could not dent this avant garde composer. A bohemian with deep roots in Odissi culture, a teacher known as an institution builder, Balakrushna Dash's school was instrumental in developing a cadre of successful music makers. He was the guru who had innovations in every composition, almost.

The industry rivalries of his times notwithstanding, his creativity was unmatched, conceded by his severest critics. Rumour mongers were more interested in scheming stories about his personal life in Calcutta and other places. But the string of hits – Nua Bou, Sadhana, Amada Bata, Adina Megha were of national character. But for the language they could have seamlessly been pan India in effect. His own renditions of 'Sanginire Rasa Ranginire (writing of 18th century poet Gopalakrushna Padavali (Patnaik) and Thaka Mana Chala Jiba (writing of 17th century poet, Saria Bhika) are considered references in Odia culture, starting from dance to drama. Former Chief Minister of Odisha and Litterateur Nandini Satpathy wrote the sleeve notes of the LP and Odisha's celebrated painter and artiste Dinanth Pathy designed the cover of the LP. Our culture carries such inspirational stories of exceptional team work in collective promotion of Odisha culture and art in various forms. Music was mentored, nurtured and coloured by Balakrushna Dash, unprecedented, independent and free spirited. I have heard this from Akshaya Mohanty that at one point Balakrushna Dash was the treat of Calcutta music scene, language agnostic. He was one of the most dominant music makers of east India – with fusion, folk and future.

Listen to Mana Manena (Nua Bou) by Shipra Bose, Nayana Sunayanare (Sadhana) by Pranab Patnaik, Aei Bhara Janha rati, Jochana Luchana and realise the depth of our tunes, even if it is filmy music. I am convinced that we are responsible for the younger generations distancing themselves from legitimate Odia music, because we have kept them away. They deserve better. They deserve to be told about the distinctive greatness of Odia music, created by the iconic Balakrushna Dash.

His music defined Odia culture.

Do we not deserve at least a Padma award on his behalf - Balakrushna Dash, the avant garde, sudhakar (source of nectar), renaissance man of Odia music? Last I saw his statue near Rabindra Mandap required repair work which we completed, as a motely group of music buffs.

Apathy & tokenism in culture is prescription for social crisis. No one in the civil society can escape.

■

The chronic Odia self-denigration

Recently I met a close friend, well-heeled Odia and with a perennially professed Odia love. I was quite shocked when the friend, mentioned in a refrain, during our conversation that "he had not found any Odia youth interesting and savvy as he has in other states". He meant lacking in chutzpah and smartness. I realise that such a mindless statement need not be overestimated or overemphasised. But it deserves to be given the importance of 'pulse reading'. Needless to mention, what ensued was my painful rebuttal, a spate of counterpoints, civil and yet heated arguments but I was re-bruised by the limitless depth of self-belittling. It is a black current from the black hole which has severely damaged our state, our language, our culture and all of us. This was asymptomatic but my learning from his thought is that most of us, unbelievably in our close proximities, nurture this 'smallness' about ourselves, quite unshakably. Over the years, I have endured many such blows, but every time it helps gather myself to a denser activism. The taunt works well. These sleeper cells exist in the well placed gentry of our state. My rural family, my country siblings are far more dedicated activists for the state than the white collar self-doubters. I feel deceived because these naysayers, with the required wherewithal, defeat the credulous champions who are powerless. It is the trusting believers versus the deep-slaying misanthropes. Can any society pull itself up with this negative force at the top? Is it possible to create an Atmanirbhar Odisha with this corrosive mind-set?

The governments can go on presenting public schemes for public good. But the demand for these schemes, the internalisation of the beneficiaries, and the sum total of welfare measures will always remain unmatched to the operational efforts. The defeatism among general mass buries all initiatives. The lethal poison of self-doubt kills more people than any army or war. When the self is gone, how can we plan for self-reliance (Atmanirbhar)?

It is imminent that we kick off a large scale program on Odia mind-set change, in the state and among the diaspora. This should be a rigorous community based program in the lines of behaviour change initiatives in health sector interventions. Faith in one's self and fellow selves (the society) is the biggest upliftment charter for all of us. Each one of us should be responsible for developing the self-esteem of minimum 10 youngsters in our circles – from IT hubs & diaspora to migrants and own siblings and children. I should speak to my child first. Odia evangelism should begin at home. Spread the word around about Odisha, its legacy, the scopes it offers and the bonding it can forge to contribute to the national GDP and national character. We are a land of comity, amity and soft power, but should be result and evidence backed.

There should be regular, well researched webinars on "know your own land'. This series should invite youths from all districts in phased manner to participate. They in turn would replicate the series among their cohorts. Information purely based on WhatsApp University does not help. Seniors should mentor the next generations.

The civil society has to take up cudgels to brighten its outlook. Rapid industrialisation, exposure of global events, international achievements of young Odias, and increase in income and opportunities, nothing has been able to lower the trepidations of Odia self-pity, as desired. Our social balance sheet flaunts assets which no other state in India, can even dream of. But who cares to gather and construct narratives for the state?

The governments are doing their best in terms of offerings. But without any social encouragement, support or complementarity. I often wonder how lonely governments must be in their solitary efforts. The policy makers and the civil servants have no support from us, the civil society. Is the civil society only meant to draw benefits without any responsibilities? Am I only to demean my fellow Odias without doing anything to ameliorate the status? I take all benefits from the state, go out, place myself well and then snigger with aplomb. Do I deserve to address it as 'my state'?

Undoubtedly explanations for economic growth should be broadened to include cultural determinants. Culture has and will influence economic outcomes by affecting such personal traits as tenacity, confidence, thrift, willingness to work hard, and openness to strangers. Our openness to strangers is actually skewed, sometimes too cosy for comfort.

We need not be obtrusive and loud but at the same time there is no need to consider self as ingénue, gauche and mentally subservient. Our compassion, affability and politeness is our hallmark, the avant-garde in this world which is chasing these higher life qualities. But the foundation is our self-belief.

The state now needs to dedicate resources to translate Odia literature and scriptures into classy English and other international languages. Without translation the cultural flowering will cease, as it has for so many decades. Public libraries need to be newly built or refurbished and despite challenges in mobilising communities to utilise libraries, still the movement would create the trend. We need to create trends to entice young minds and future Odisha architects and impresarios.

University of Culture should be perfect platform to lead the Odia reactivation. All the Odia Associations, across India and outside are groups of Odia-enthusiasts and these need to be mainstreamed. Otherwise they would continue working in silos and be happy with incremental contributions. Their synergies would steer quantum jump in Odia motivation, self-esteem and productivity. Building self-esteem is a time consuming process and warrants assimilation. There is no quick fix to such renascence. Odisha's development will directly contribute to the nation's development. Our wallowing in self-pity negates the strength in our piety. Self-deprecating pulls down all of us together, including my friend, who needs urgent support in broad basing his Odia experience.

At the end of the conversation I was pitying both – him & I.

Is it due to the benediction of the Lord of the Universe or due to the ever pervading community flatness or equals as the Supreme's creation, that Puri has a distinct maverick tint in life? But it is unmistakably woven around worship and wellness, both of mind and body. There is a marked chutzpah in the air. The common address is "Mani' between senior and juniors, old and new, master and trainee, everyone and everyone. Mani in Odia is precious jewel and each soul is recognised as a Mani by the other soul and can be there be any better common manifestation of divinity. The article titled Mani, Sanyam and Divinity describes the confluence of free spirit, restrain in habits and *tathata* (oneness with existence) around us. These might sound contradictory but is 'uniquely' so. There is swag of invincibility in people born out of the discipline and rigour of wrestling, which has provided the texture of day-to-day life and has coloured the enigmatic heritage. Gopinath Mohapatra (aka Supakar) embodies quintessential Puri with the heady concoction of stamina, sanctity and nobility. His coaching of youngsters and exemplary life might sound simple but reminds of the halcyon days of physical fitness, verdure and wholeness in character.

■

Mani, *Sanyam* & Divinity in Puri

I find Puri unorthodox, very inventive and completely original. That's divinity for you, because orthodoxy is human created and dogma is human imposed. The Supreme never wants the children to be bound – would you want your children to be tied down? One can smell freedom in Puri – that is why in the 70s and 80s it was more international than it is now. We had more foreigners coming and spending long spells in Puri. The Chakratirth 'side' was known as 'foreigner side'. A place with a strong character and people with tremendous amount of self-confidence. At times quirky & cocky but Puri is always the "one and only". Visitors from all across the globe come to Puri – both for religious tourism and for beach/nature tourism, but this influx has not in the least, affected the core of Puri life. This is a powerful phenomenon. Of late we hear of instances where there are activities which are mostly tourist influenced. But otherwise Puri is identified as a place untouched by the pressures of "floating cultures". This has a flip side too but this also indicates a healthy, resolute individuality. The Odia inscriptions of the 15th Century A.D. called the place Purusottama Kataka and if the "Ideal Man" resides in this place then the life of this place has to be concomitantly ideal and idyllic. Interestingly the inhabitants of Puri strongly believe in this. They are 'family' with the Lord, not supplicants forever.

Life starts much before sunrise at about 4-4.30 in the morning at the Jegaghar. Jegaghar is the local club where the seniors mentor the wards in disciplined pursuit of wrestling, body building & gymnastics. Even today when all the sports mentioned above are on the wane in other parts of the country, Puri lads, in the teeth of the changing times are not ashamed of flaunting their practice of 1000 dandas (push-ups), 25kms running (jogging in the beach sand), 1000 baithiks (squats), hours of wrestling practice in specially prepared wrestling space in fine soil (with liberal portions of clay). Rest of India holds this in awe. It is not only about physical exercise and workouts. I know of masters who live there (in Jegaghars) even if they are from the same sahi (locality) or from the town. Besides wrestling other activities like practicing classical music, instruments like Pakhawaj (similar to the Mridangam in southern India), vegetable colour dyeing of gamuchas (loin cloths), painting in Pattas or other medium have been common in these hubs. The subject matter of Patta Chitra is mostly folk based & mythological. So the jegaghars are Community Centers which were started as gymnasiums and but have expanded over time to become mostly learning centers of various arts, crafts and skills. But the women of the society do not have much access to Jegaghars, as the responsibility of providing physical security and safeguarding the society was deemed as primarily a man's job. Young boys choosing to go to Jegaghars are accorded special status or a tacit appreciation by the elders and the peers. Jegaghars are the erstwhile barracks

& training grounds for soldiers (paikas). Some of the important sahis of Puri (I dare not miss others because there is a strong competition between the jegaghars of different sahis) are Bali sahi, Dolamandapa sahi, Goudabada sahi, Harachandi sahi, Kundeibenta sahi, Baddei sahi, Balagandi sahi, Baseli sahi, Ganamala sahi, Gooria sahi, Gurruntee Haragouri sahi, Kalikadebi sahi, Karati sahi, Kapal mochana, Khatua sahi, Khuntia sahi, Kumuti sahi, Manikarnika sahi, Mausima, Pathuria sahi, Patna Jenapur, Patna Jagannathpur, Patna Balabhadra Ballava, Patna Matipada, Patna Balisahi, Patna Parrhee sahi, Patna Kumbharpada, Patna Tikarpada and Talichha sahi. Each sahi inhabitant is extremely loyal to his/her Jega, in the same vein as the loyalty to English premier football clubs. One example of a classic and continuing Jega is one called Panchamukhi Jega in Markandeswar Sahi. Started on April 14th, 1962, this jega was patronized by Late Sri Raghunath Supakar, he an accomplished wrestler always maintaining a body weight in the range of 50-52 kgs till he passed away at the age of 70. Till his last he was always seen working out with boys one-third his age and also floating in water for hours together, doing various asanas in water demonstrating tremendous breath control. Known to be a strict disciplinarian he would not even allow his wards to come to the Jega without proper haircut. I have met him during my growing up years and have always been overawed by his disciplined lifestyle, mental and physical strength. The culture of Puri is not *bhang*-centric as has been generalized & trivialised by people who do not have interest in deeper study of the nuances of life in Puri. There are 62 Jegaghars in Puri, churning out on an average about 50 wrestlers each in a year. All this with strong local, sahi patronage and without much support from the government. And during the famous Sahi Jatras, a designated Jegaghar would lead the procession with pride and grandeur. There is a euphoria around physical fitness and strength unparalleled in Odisha and rare in India. This has happened much before the dramatized versions of WWE/WWF sweeping us away in the idiot boxes. Such is the level of significance given to good life practices in Puri. And this social norm is deeply entrenched.

According to Cunningham the ancient name of the town was Charitra. So relevant. Puri echoes character, Charitra.

The jegaghars are in seven sahis (sata sahis) and all the seven sahis have four headmen designated as Sahi Naik. Today with the changes in the local municipal and urban governance, the Sahi Naiks still call the shots. The brilliance of Puri is in hosting global travellers and yet not diluting the local culture and way of life. I have heard that once the legendary Pandit Omkarnath Thakur was taking an early morning stroll and was passing by a Jegaghar when he heard spellbinding Pakhwaj play by a young boy. When he asked him about the source of his skill and who his master was, the boy without realising whom he was talking replied matter-of-fact that there was nothing great in what he was doing and that he does this every day because he was just copying his father, who played like this always, without much hullabaloo. Pandit realized the deep-seated culture of the place and is reported to have acclaimed that the boy was playing extraordinary music and if that was common play in Puri, the place deserves to be saluted. The people of Puri love pets and many households have cats, parrots and other varieties of birds as pets. I know of many sevayats of the Jagannath temple always carrying birds perched on their fingers and walking with almost a superman gait and sometimes talking in a foreign language like Nepali or Burmese. They know the languages through their interactions with their clientele, spread out. I am sure, the peculiarities emanate from a sense of total surrender to the Almighty. They strongly believe that the Lord is their brother and that the Lord would take care of them, come what may. They are family members of the Lord and because they are in a sense of total surrender, they are free from worldly worries and that is why they can pursue hobbies like Pets, Music, cooking and the like. This attitude might not be appreciated by many but certainly deserves a better understanding before being dismissed as plain arrogance or irreverence.

Lagom in Sweden signifies balanced living or knowing limitations in our everyday life "Not too little. Not too much. Just right.", Hygge in Denmark philosophy denotes 'coziness of the soul', and Fika, the significance of taking regular breaks during work. Puri Jegaghar culture nurtures Sanyam (8   /   .   in hindi) or restrain in our lives.

It is not for nothing that commonly people address each other as *"mani"* with a swag in Puri. Mani means precious jewel. That's the esteem for each soul in Puri.

■

When do politicians get to think?

Presently in India, the working style of politicians is fast changing. Physical proximity to the people or the constituents is diminishing in importance. Regular issues of people or the 'area problems' are somewhat distant. About a year before and a year after electioneering, the politician is typically clued into the area nitty gritty. The bigger the profile, the higher the aloofness. A parliamentarian friend justifying his absence from the constituency once remarked "if I go once in a while in a big vehicle for a ribbon-cutting ceremony in my area, and mouth only English, I am considered, the babu. Otherwise it's the man next door." We have come a long way In seventy-three years. The difference between rural and urban India is blurring. Social media does the midwifery to a large extent, both ways. Politicians speak to general mass, growingly through social media. In the next five years about 70% of India would be on social media or social networks. The rest 30% would either belong to the category of secondary targets of communication (majorly informed by the 70%) or would be literally inconsequential in real responsive terms. By the end of the next government term, 2030, the outreach intensity of an average Indian politician would no more be weighing upon his/her performance. The hangover of COVID effect would keep the neta away from constituency till about 2021 and for a few more years after than the hangover would provide the alibi to stay away from area (read constituency).

It is a paradox, how the peoples' representatives have drifted away from the people. But do people complain? I guess not. In the next general elections, more and more candidates would have public debates among themselves and less of house-to-house canvassing. The pressure of first line solutions to community issues will increase for the civil servants.

Would that leave more time for the politician to think about innovations, about creative ways of managing India's development, devising out-of-the-box policy templates and drives? I have been watching politicians from close quarters and all kinds – the non-english speaking, the foreign educated, the dynasts, the self-made, the honest changemakers, the make-believe changemakers. All of them are running all the time and hardly spend time in lateral thinking or futuristic envisioning. The leader-like intuition and 'large picture view' is getting rarefied in leaders. Winning elections is not leadership. It might be a part of it but I continue to advocate for representation with or without office.

For example, Sansad Adarsh Gram Yojana (SAGY), a pathbreaking scheme to enable Parliamentarians to implement and demonstrate innovations in rural development, has been a laggard. The Rural Development ministry in a review has observed that SAGY has not made "any perceptible impact" and the villages selected under it cannot be called 'model (adarsh) villages)". Preparation of Village development Plans and creation of development clusters is far below expectations. It is a common experience that the youths in the villages are getting more and more alienated from the mainstream development process. So, who would eventually lead whom? Leadership should not be reduced to a rigmarole. Have the voters assumed that choosing candidates is almost folderol and that their own involvement in the social and governance processes is avoidable. In this medley the dream of a $5 trillion economy or 'make in India' or Atmanirbhar Bharat suffer and fail to drive our collective solidarity. Are only the party or government supremos supposed to think creatively? Have the rest of the cohorts lost their energy, interest and have become drifters. If only CMs and PMs of the country were to drive everything then why is the rest of the cabinet or party organisations necessary? Despite challenges we as a democracy are unique in the world – tenacious with unparallel diversity and ultimately Gandhians. Why don't our politicians spend time thinking on development, beyond regular political machinations, day-to-day firefighting for protecting turfs and doling out favours to a few acolytes or hapless voters who can somehow access them. Voters meeting with their leaders is a great occasion for celebration for the entire village. It is a big & special event to have an audience with the leader. But otherwise, I have seen leaders super busy but doing nothing constructive. They are so occupied that they have to get by on a few hours' sleep. I often wonder, does sleep affect their functioning? And I know in many cases sleep deprivation has contributed to some of the mistakes and gaffes. Researchers say that getting fewer than six hours of sleep a night on a regular basis "is inadequate to sustain health.

There is evidence that suggests that brief naps (ideally no longer than 20 minutes) can enhance alertness and performance. Our politicians, cutting across regions or power base, do not have time for even "power naps." The need to have better time management to enhance their productivity. Good for them and good for all of us.

Mostly they are driven by the orders of the high command or the head quarter. But 90% of running those errands have hardly anything to do with their own constituencies. We suppose that in a fiercely competitive political firmament the politicians would be more immersed or guarded in the development of their own constituencies and giving less time to other 'peripheral works'. But this indicates another syndrome – their full dependency on the party or the supremo to win elections for them. In the meantime, they have become complacent. Their boss or their symbol would get them votes. As a result, in the last few years, 'supremo' has become a buzzword for all parties. The 'supremo' is ascending in invincibility and inaccessibility. In fact, more the remoteness, higher is his or her stature. This trend would not buck as long as the politicians continue to drift in the largesse of a party ticket or the 'blessings' of the boss. The basic objective of his or her being in politics is not met, if it was ever anything else other than enjoying the pelf and power without responsibility.

They choose to be vassals because it is comfortable and rewarding. This builds undue pressure on the party chief or head of the government. Because everything flows from his/her office and is vulnerable to targeting and maligning. Obviously, the party or government head turns more totalitarian. But that helps the entire state or the country machinery run. Most of the rest of the party or the cabal is freeloading. About 75 per cent of MPs in the Lok Sabha have at least a graduate degree, while 10 per cent are only matriculates. But qualifications aside, what stops them from thinking? Ideating about development in a way which will help us face the RCEP clique, or the 1.5R" C temp rise cap under Paris agreement or the preparedness for the SDG Investor Map (promoting investment opportunity areas, IOAs). The primary role of the representative is to bridge the gap between policy and population, between macro and micro, between legislation and implementation.

When do politicians get to plan their contribution to a better India? They are perpetually engaged in chores which should be ideally handled with the help of their teams – constituency matters – which translate to recommendation for jobs, transfers, posting, preferences in bookings, individual or community litigations etc. They should concentrate on policy making, situational assessment of livelihoods, welfare activities, development project(s) ideation, proposal preparations and proactive constituency development in the lines of competitive federalism. Some MPs who do that have successfully established a firm and consistent electoral base. Someone had famously said that "voters don't decide issues, they decide who will decide issues."

Good vison makes good politics.

A politician in our country continues to be the hope for the last house at the last mile. S/he has challenges of capacities and the politicisation of the environment doesn't encourage many volunteers to be a part of the circle and help the politician think different and think big. There is a misconception that needs to be cleared. It is not that voters won't approve of big vision. They are not as short term or inveterate favour seekers as they are made out to be. I agree with the observation which says "show me the heroes that the youth of your country look up to, and I will tell you the future of your country."

The child begging on the traffic stop should be rescued, the girl should be in college, the youth should be working, and you should be managing all of this, the country.

All of us are waiting for you to think and act. Take time out for us.

∎

Why are we scared of tribals?

(This article is co-authored by Gadadhar Parida, Director Tribal Museum, & Charudutta Panigrahi, Author. Taking up cudgels on behalf of the indigenous communities, both the activists urge the civil society to protect their indigenous families facing the onslaught of inhuman greed and extreme apathy. Our own indigenous families staring at extinction.)

We (you, I and them) are all tribals by origin. Over the years we have lied to ourselves and conveniently believed that we are not tribals and that we were never tribals. A repeated lie becomes the truth. In the last seven decades and more, after many 'convenient' map makings, we are trying our best to destroy tribals and their lives. Still they hold the key to our rental economy, specifically for Odisha, Jharkhand, Chhattisgarh, parts of AP, Maharashtra, and the North East. The platitudes related to trillion USD economy is majorly based on the mines and minerals under the custody of our indigenous families . The tribals, whom we left behind and set out in pursuit of creature comforts, remain the guardian of flora and fauna, below which lie the sparkle of billions of dollars. In our interest, we have ensured that they get relegated to be defined as 'backward communities' so that we can intervene the paradise with our largesse, which we think they need but they know they don't. This is quite akin to our rushing back to our village paternal property, for an emergency bail out, when we are chocked in debt-ridden city existence. Déjà vu.

It is growingly becoming chaotic in tribal communities in mineral haven, Koraput. The haven has attracted ravens. We (you and I) have been successful in finally 'breaking' them. If we do not make cohesive communities fritter away, we will be rendered jobless, penniless, and worthless. For example, the NGO sector has to play the tribal story, year after year, for their donors to keep them alive. Jargons like 'capacity building' and 'community empowerment' are their lifeline. Sporadic cases of tribal 'development' or tribal youth making big is media-hyped so much that it is like being euphoric, taking a selfie with a chimpanzee.

There has always been a disciplined and organised leadership style in the community, till we tampered and wrecked the indigenous society. A new village was typically established as Ektaguda – which literally means a village discovered by one person. The word 'Ekta' here does not signify unity but 'singular'. When there is any calamity in a village, people tend to shift to a new place because they believe that they have incurred wrath of their deity. Any community adversity like an epidemic or village fire or ill health of children is bad omen and the elders in the community are convinced that the deity wants them to abandon the village. Accordingly, the enterprising of the lot, the Columbus, ventures out to find a new place. He explores, discovers, starts the settlement and becomes the obvious choice for the village Headman. He becomes the

Nayak and the system becomes hereditary. This system of village administration need not fit into our description of governance but it always provided the three crucial elements – i) unbridled independence to villagers including exemplary gender equality ii) community living with no individual asset holding and iii) collective livelihoods mechanisms like community farming. The indigenous communities thus are much more united and bonded than we are. We should envy, obviously. With technologies we have further divided ourselves and all our algorithms are aimed at profiling, dividing and creating a new world of fakes. Our divisibility exposes our hypothetical 'mainstream' - where there is hardly any stream and there is nothing called a 'main' because there is unruly wrangling for freedom. USA to Belarus, about 25% of our time is spent on streets protesting and still we bracket indigenous people as PVTG – Particularly Vulnerable Tribal Groups. Who is vulnerable? You know the truth.

ଚେଇଁ ଶୋଇବ ଯିଏ ତାକୁ ଉଠାଇବ କିଏ ?– this is an Odia saying whose literal translation could be something like " who can nudge to wake up someone who pretends to be sleeping while awake?".

Our machinations have brought in complications in their lives. Gender based violence was never known in the indigenous communities because there was never any segregation – because there was no individual property or family entitlements or self-imposed, hypocritical rituals of fidelity. It was simple commune living. Many of our Gurus later on replicated commune living in western countries which has been hailed as 'magic'. But we, with the help of statutes are bent on obliterating pristine life in its most original form. We were always meant to be like this. Crime against women, burglary, cheating was never known in the communities. They did not use money and did not have any need for lust. All their needs were met by their Supreme, their forests—perennial streams, abundance of fruits, spices, mushrooms, wild tubers, roots. The mix of native millets, pulses, legumes, and oil seeds grown on small shift-and-burn patches on hill slopes, locally known as dongar (the clear patches) made their diets super healthy. Non communicable, lifestyle diseases were not known, as recent as a few years ago. They depended on the valley – the outside market for cloth, salt, kerosene, and the delicacy of dried fish, intermittently. They had everything and so did not ever need money. We are jealous, quite naturally. We are poverty stricken but we run programs to eradicate their poverty. Hopeless sadism and nauseous guile. I and my civil society are squarely responsible.

With our public schemes and the lure of money, the community became political. Today the community leaders are trained to engage in bitter, schismatic, and corrupt governance. We need them and so we penetrated their self-sustained system, created artificial needs, peddled "development', and finally got them addicted to our tokenism.

Tokenism is the new opiate of life. We have successfully spiked credulous lives with the poison of deceitful politics. If development was well meaning, then there was no place for politics. Why do we have tribal youths going out as migrant labour? In the last seven decades and more how many community livelihoods programs have provided sustainability to the indigenous communities? Where is the mainstream/ Do you see that animal anywhere?

Is holding a smart phone, riding a bike, or getting glued to porn in the name of OTT, development? The ward member in a village has all the whereabouts of girls being trafficked out of the village or youths getting into organised crimes. How do we sensitise the ward member that due to his or her complicity, a whole generation in getting wiped out? Do our civil society organisations go and spend time with the community leaders? Do our Harvard heading 'smart fellows in public policy and governance' care to work with them? Do we discuss threadbare the issues of the communities in our endless, wisdom spewing Zoom meetings? Talking and talking and talking we achieve nirvana. While post-retirement wisdom is flowing unchecked, the extraction industry has already extracted our native lives from us, natives.

Some day we will realise, if we are left alive and soon the forest Lord will seek abode in another planet. Mythologies are no more myths – I am the *asura* and am scared of tribals because I am lowly.

Ode to Thy Spirit!

Looking through the panes,
I saw Mirza,
Trudging with one more wish,
To keep on crafting,
With dreams,
A bouquet of many more wishes!

With my eyes open,
With my enslaved moments,
Without me,
I see him,
Still winking,
& looking back.......

(**Background:** I saw Mirza walking down a rain lashed Bhubaneswar, may be in the road in front of Trident or right in front of Bhubaneswar Club. It was early evening, the early dusk lights on in the city, the skyline with a mix of crimson and indigo, completely drenched in a flowing white robe Mirza was murmuring something and walking.I ran upto him, asked him for a cup of tea with leaking rain drops in a roadside shop, he smiled and said "I would keep on coming and see you next time". You are a peddler, I said and and groped for the switch to put on Lennon's Yesterday. It was dark evening with deafening rain drops. With me was the waft of Bhubaneswar Baula trees drenched in love. We had a great time !)

Say AUM Jagannath instead of JAI Jagannath

The greetings of Odias or Odisha-philes should be AUM Jagannath in place of JAI Jagannath. Recently I was giving a talk in Delhi where I mooted AUM and it was well taken. Jagannath is the Lord of the Cosmos and the MahaVishnu. One interpretation of MahaVishnu is that since the first sound of existence emanated from Ratnasinghasan or the seat of the Lord, in the sanctum sanctorum of Puri temple, the Lord is All and so MahaVishnu. AUM, the primordial sound rose from Him. Jagannath hence is an avataree and not an avatar – the highest and only IS and not a manifestation.

Jai Jagannath is 'glory to the Lord' and this address has no depth in it. Over a period of time it has become a flippantly used, common prefix. There is no gravity in singing the glory of the MahaVishnu, without reminiscing the original hum of existence. Every time you say OM Jagannath, it cleans you from inside. With Jagannath we need to attach a meaningful and pristine explanation. The adjective has to have insight, divinity and panache. OM or

AUM has all of that. I don't have to sing the glory of the Lord or supplement to His glory. He is every-thing and every no-thing. So, what is this glory we are talking about? And Jai could also mean victory. What victory of the Lord? Is He fighting? Rather, the word Jai reduces the glory of the Lord. Every time you say OM Jagannath, it touches the nerve of Jagannath benediction.

If you are alert, you would realise that the word Jai is flat. It lacks the intensity that should be accorded to the Lord of Existence. How do we bring in new waves of Jagannath consciousness if we do not form our invocations in a manner in which we touch the essence? The essence is OM.

Without diluting the core Jagannath elements, the address should help in developing resilience in consciousness. Because in Odisha, Jagannath consciousness is the state culture's wherewithal and capacity to maintain and develop a distinct cultural identity, knowledge and practices.

He is Purna Brahma: In Jagannath Charitamruta, a work of post Panchasakha Period, (1470-1550 A.D), Lord Jagannath has been described as the Supreme Lord or Purna Brahma, or the "Whole" of the Cosmos. Purna Brahman means the Absolute which engulfs everything which we call creation. There is no Truth superior to Him.

He is Avataree: Sarala Dasa, has expressed that all the Avataras or the descents of Vishnu manifest from Lord Jagannath and merge into Him after their cosmic plays. Achutyananda Das in his Sunya Samhita writes that all the ten incarnations emanate from this Daru Brahma and are again dissolved in Him. He is Avataree and MahaVishnu. Ramanuj Acharya in the twelfth century preached the doctrine of visista advaitavad and regarded Lord Jagannath as Maha-Vishnu.

He is Sunya Purusha - Void Personified or a Whole which is existential and non-existential. According to the Panchsakhas, Jagannath is Sunya Purusha, Nirakar (formless) and Niranjan (mystic) – The Lord of the Universe is both Adi Sankara's Advaita Brahman and Mahayanic Sunya.

The Lord is MahaVishnu and He is also Mahabhairav.

In the Tantric tradition, the Lord is worshiped with the bija mantra or the root incantation "klim" and sits on the Kali yantra as Daksina kalika. He is considered the Bhairava of Vimala, who is the Bhairavi:

There are innumerable references, citation, descriptions, statements, hymns, all trying to decipher the Lord of the Lords and the Lord of the Cosmos and His mystic ways.

He remains ineffable and indescribable.

Lord of the Cosmos is everything and every nothing and He belongs to All, enshrined in enigma.

Odisha has what the world covets for and why are we handling them superficially?

"Sarba Rahasya Purusottamasya

Deva Na Janati Kuta Manusya." Kapila Samhita

The mystery of Lord Jagannath is unfathomable to the Devas; and what to speak of man!

He is the Centre: The Lord is the epicentre and he rests at the navel of the Conch, the Sankha Khetra, which is a daksinavarta sankha (a special Lakshmi conch shell with the hollow part on the right side) with some part submerged under the sea. The Lord being at the navel is meaningful. Navel is the area of the body which represents the Manipura Chakra (which means "lustrous gem."). Chakra is the Sanskrit word Chakra which literally translates to wheel or disk. In yoga, meditation, and Ayurveda, this term refers to wheels of energy throughout the body. This invisible energy, called Prana, is vital life force, which keeps us vibrant, healthy, and alive. The navel or the Manipura chakra functions as an energy generator and radiates the energy.

He is Aum: The Ratna Singhasana, is the 'seed' of the Universe, the core. The core is always silent and hence Mahapurusha Vidya refers Ratna Singhasana as the Primordial sound, the Aum or the Pranava. Mmm, the humming sound of a bee, is the Pranava mantra. This is believed to be the sound of our Pranan or breathing. Therefore, it is called Pranava - the sound of breathing. And Pranava is the root mantra of Aum. The whole universe is created from "Aum." After the deluge at Bata Krishna, when the Lord again decides to create, "Aum" is heard. Thus, everything has its origin in "Aum." The syllable Om has significance not only in Hinduism but in other religions and cultures, including Buddhism, Sikhism, Jainism, besides Indonesian and Nepalese cultures. Before Creation began, there was an empty void, which was then filled with the vibrations of the sound of Aum, believed to be a manifestation of the Supreme Lord. There is complete 'quietness' in Ratna Singhasana or Ratna Vedi and this is a unique situation where a throne and primordial sound co-exist with the blessings of the Lord.

Amidst the 'surround' of silence and the absoluteness of Aum, Ratna Singhasana is the lotus. Let us get centred in life. To be consciously centred is to be in Jagannath.

Let's value our blessed birth and our possession of Universe's only precious benediction – Jagannath.

From now on,
It is no more JAI JAGANNATH.
It is forever, AUM JAGANNATH.

■

BLACK EAGLE BOOKS

www.blackeaglebooks.org
info@blackeaglebooks.org

Black Eagle Books, an independent publisher, was founded as a nonprofit organization in April, 2019. It is our mission to connect and engage the Indian diaspora and the world at large with the best of works of world literature published on a collaborative platform, with special emphasis on foregrounding Contemporary Classics and New Writing.

www.ingramcontent.com/pod-product-compliance
Lightning Source LLC
Chambersburg PA
CBHW031059080526
44587CB00011B/741